W9-CCW-442

J.R.R. TOLKIEN

Recent Titles in Greenwood Biographies

J. K. Rowling: A Biography
Connie Ann Kirk

The Dalai Lama: A Biography
Patricia Cronin Marcello

Margaret Mead: A Biography
Mary Bowman-Kruhm

J.R.R. TOLKIEN

A Biography

Leslie Ellen Jones

GREENWOOD BIOGRAPHIES

GREENWOOD PRESS

WESTPORT, CONNECTICUT · LONDON

Library of Congress Cataloging-in-Publication Data

Jones, Leslie, 1959–
    J. R. R. Tolkien : a biography / Leslie Ellen Jones.
        p. cm.—(Greenwood Press biography series, ISSN 1540–4900)
    Includes bibliographical references (p.) and index.
    ISBN 0–313–32340–2 (alk. paper)
    1. Tolkien, J. R. R. (John Ronald Reuel), 1892–1973. 2. Oxford (England)—
Intellectual life—20th century. 3. Authors, English—20th century—Biography.
4. Anglicists—Great Britain—Biography. 5. Fantasy literature—Authorship.
6. Middle Earth (Imaginary place) 7. Oxford (England)—Biography. 8. Inklings
(Group of writers) I. Title. II. Series.
PR6039.O32 Z6616   2003
828'.91209—dc21
[B]   2002032074

British Library Cataloguing in Publication Data is available.

Library of Congress Catalog Card Number: 2002032074
ISBN: 0–313–32340–2
ISSN: 1540–4900

First published in 2003

Greenwood Press, 88 Post Road West, Westport, CT 06881
An imprint of Greenwood Publishing Group, Inc.
www.greenwood.com

Printed in the United States of America

The paper used in this book complies with the
Permanent Paper Standard issued by the National
Information Standards Organization (Z39.48–1984).

10 9 8 7 6 5 4 3 2 1

CONTENTS

Photo essay follows page 77.

SERIES FOREWORD

In response to high school and public library needs, Greenwood developed this distinguished series of full-length biographies specifically for student use. Prepared by field experts and professionals, these engaging biographies are tailored for high school students who need challenging yet accessible biographies. Ideal for secondary school assignments, the length, format, and subject areas are designed to meet educators' requirements and students' interests.

Greenwood offers an extensive selection of biographies spanning all curriculum-related subject areas including social studies, the sciences, literature and the arts, history and politics, as well as popular culture, covering public figures and famous personalities from all time periods and backgrounds, both historic and contemporary, who have made an impact on American and/or world culture. Greenwood biographies were chosen based on comprehensive feedback from librarians and educators. Consideration was given to both curriculum relevance and inherent interest. The result is an intriguing mix of the well known and the unexpected, the saints and sinners from long-ago history and contemporary pop culture. Readers will find a wide array of subject choices from fascinating crime figures like Al Capone to inspiring pioneers like Margaret Mead, from the greatest minds of our time like Stephen Hawking to the most amazing success stories of our day like J.K. Rowling.

While the emphasis is on fact, not glorification, the books are meant to be fun to read. Each volume provides in-depth information about the subject's life from birth through childhood, the teen years, and adulthood. A thorough account relates family background and education, traces personal and professional influences, and explores struggles, accomplishments, and contributions. A timeline highlights the most significant life events against a historical perspective. Suggestions for further reading give the biographies added reference value.

ACKNOWLEDGMENTS

Thanks are due to my parents, Bob and Louise Jones, for buying me a new computer when a glass of wine destroyed the hard drive of my laptop in the middle of chapter six; to Karen Burgess of the Center for Medieval and Renaissance Studies at UCLA, for sharing with me her personal archive of Tolkien-related magazine articles from the 1960s; and to my cats, Finn and Dahlia, for heroically sprawling all over the sofa so that I had no option but to sit at the desk and write.

INTRODUCTION

Perhaps the most remarkable aspect of John Ronald Reuel Tolkien's epic *Lord of the Rings* is the degree to which its author succeeded in his goal of creating a fantasy world that nonetheless appears to be completely real. Its languages, legends, history, and geography are as realistic—and sometimes as bizarre—as those of the world inhabited by Tolkien's readers, and for many of them, the reason the trilogy remains with them long after its covers have been closed is that they can continue to inhabit it beyond the boundaries of the tale. It is hard to believe that such a fully realized world could simply have been *created* by a single individual; surely it must have some external foundation, surely he was, as he sometimes claimed, merely a historian of a lost and ancient time rather than its author.

Tolkien was not only an author, but also a scholar of ancient languages and literatures. The narratives among which he spent his academic career were so old that the names of their authors were lost. The most one could hope for was to identify a poet's locale by the dialect in which he wrote, or perhaps to identify his education by his literary allusions. Not surprisingly, therefore, Tolkien himself was of the opinion that knowledge of an author's biography was not necessary for an understanding of his works. It is also true that knowing the intimate details of an author's life—even those as heavily documented as contemporary authors are, who live in an age of paperwork and Internet trails—still cannot completely explain an individual's genius, or explain why certain events inspired one artist to write reams of elaborate fantasy, while another produced precisely five exquisite sonnets, and another delved into gritty realism.

Nonetheless, an account of an author's life can identify some of the raw material of inspiration; it can explain why an author wrote voluminously, or sporadically; it can help readers understand the process of writing and thus appreciate the author's achievement in wrestling his material into a seemingly seamless form. It can illustrate the way in which an individual takes the stuff of living and turns it into art.

John Ronald Reuel Tolkien was born on January 3, 1892, in Bloemfontein, South Africa, and died on September 2, 1973, in Bournemouth, England. The world changed a lot during his lifetime—he was born more than a decade before the Wright Brothers' first heavier-than-air flight at Kitty Hawk and died four years after the first man walked on the moon; he grew up in the waning days of the Victorian era and died along with Swinging London; he was an officer in World War I, while two of his sons served in World War II. He came of age along with the automobile and saw enough of what it did to the environment to decide that he did not want to have one any longer.

Tolkien was also the agent of some small but significant changes in his world. He persuaded his fellow professors to change the requirements for a degree in English so that generations of Oxford students graduated with a first-hand reading knowledge of Old English literature rather than simply learning an abstract history of the English language. He championed the reading of medieval English texts as literature—as narratives that were told by real people to real people because they were exciting and entertaining stories—rather than as dusty linguistic archives to be mined for random facts supporting a scholar's pet theory about the development of weaponry or the lingering remnants of paganism. Most importantly, however, he almost single-handedly revived the genre of adult fantasy fiction, which had fallen into disrepute against the more glamorous technological allurements of science fiction. He did so by writing stories that were completely new, set in a world he himself had created, but whose themes and structure grew not out of the modern novel but the epics, myths, and legends of medieval Europe.

There is perhaps a unifying theme in these accomplishments: Tolkien believed in stories. He was trained as a philologist, as a historian of individual words, but what really interested him was how those words were strung together to tell a tale. He wanted his students to appreciate the tale-telling of the ancient Saxons and Icelanders, so he taught them how to read the languages in which those tales were captured. Language was not an abstract concept for him; language only existed to the extent that there were people to read it or speak it—to tell stories in it. He played at inventing his own languages, and inevitably, he had to create stories to use those languages. The story of his life, therefore, is the story of his work, both professional and private.

TIMELINE

1892   John Ronald Reuel Tolkien born January 3 in Bloemfontein, South Africa

1894   Hilary Arthur Reuel Tolkien born in Bloemfontein, South Africa

1895   Mabel Tolkien takes her sons back to Birmingham, England, for a family visit; Arthur Tolkien remains in Africa

1896   Arthur Tolkien dies of hemorrhage resulting from rheumatic fever February 15; Mabel Tolkien and sons move to Sarehole Mill, outside Birmingham, in the summer

1900   Mabel Tolkien and her sons convert to Catholicism; move back to the Birmingham suburb of Moseley to be near a Catholic church; JRRT begins to attend King Edward's School

1901   The Tolkiens move from Moseley to King's Heath

1902   The Tolkiens move from King's Heath to Oliver Road, Edgbaston; the boys are enrolled at St. Philip's Grammar School, attached to the Birmingham Oratory; the Tolkiens are befriended by Father Francis Morgan

1903   The Tolkien boys leave St. Philip's and JRRT is re-enrolled at King Edward's School on a scholarship

1904   Mabel Tolkien is diagnosed with diabetes and spends time in the hospital; the family spends the summer at the Birmingham Oratory's house at Rednal; Mabel Tolkien dies of complications of diabetes on November 14

1905   JRRT and Hilary move in with their recently widowed Aunt Beatrice in Stirling Road

1908   JRRT and Hilary move to Mrs. Faulkener's house on Duchess Road, where their fellow lodger is Edith Bratt

1909   Father Morgan discovers the romance between JRRT and Edith; JRRT fails to win a scholarship to Oxford

1910   JRRT and Hilary move to lodgings a few streets away from the Faulkener house; Edith moves to Cheltenham to lodge with the Jessops; JRRT wins an exhibition to Exeter College, Oxford, in December

1911   Formation of the T.C.B.S., including JRRT, Christopher Wiseman, R. Q. Gilson, and G. B. Smith; JRRT finishes school in June, takes a holiday with his brother, Aunt Jane, and others in Switzerland; matriculates at Oxford in the fall

1913   On his twenty-first birthday, JRRT writes to Edith proposing marriage; on discovering that she is engaged to another, he visits Cheltenham and successfully persuades her to break the engagement; gets a Second Class on his Honours Moderations in February and switches from classics to English; in the summer he makes a disastrous visit to France with a Mexican family

1914   Edith converts to Catholicism in January and the pair is formally engaged; JRRT spends the summer in Cornwall; World War I breaks out in the fall, but JRRT determines to finish his degree before joining up; in December, the core T.C.B.S. of Tolkien, Wiseman, Gilson, and Smith meet for what will be the last time

1915   JRRT receives a First Class Honours degree; is commissioned in the Lancashire Fusiliers; begins training in Bedford and Staffordshire

1916   JRRT and Edith are married on March 22; Tolkien is sent to France in June as signaling officer for his battalion; participates in the Battle of the Somme (July–November), during which Gilson and Smith are both killed; is invalided home in November with trench fever

1917   JRRT convalesces at Great Haywood and begins writing a mythology of "Middle-earth;" he spends much of the year in and out of the hospital; eldest son, John Francis Reuel, is born in November

1918   JRRT is discharged from the army; the family moves to Oxford, where he begins work for the *Oxford English Dictionary*

1919   JRRT begins to supplement his income with tutoring; the family moves to 1 Alfred Street

1920   JRRT is appointed Reader in English Literature at Leeds University; son Michael Hilary Reuel is born in October

1922   E. V. Gordon, whom JRRT had tutored at Oxford, joins the English Department at Leeds; he and JRRT begin work on an edition of *Sir Gawain and the Green Knight*

1924   JRRT is made Professor of English Language at Leeds; son Christopher Reuel is born in November

1925   *Sir Gawain and the Green Knight* is published; JRRT is named Rawlinson and Bosworth Professor of Anglo-Saxon at Oxford; the family moves into a house at 22 Northmoor Road

1926   JRRT befriends C. S. Lewis; formation of the Old Norse study group, the Coalbiters

1929   Daughter Priscilla Mary Reuel is born

1930   The Tolkiens move next door to 20 Northmoor Road; JRRT begins writing *The Hobbit*

1933   An informal literary club formed by Oxford undergraduate Edward Tangye Lean, the Inklings, dissolves when Tangye Lean leaves university, but Tolkien and Lewis carry on the name and the discussion on their own as an outgrowth of the Coalbiters, with a varying cast of fellows over the years, including Owen Barfield, J. A. W. Bennett, Lord David Cecil, Nevill Coghill, Jim Dundas-Grant, Hugo Dyson, Adam Fox, Colin Hardie, R. E. Havard, Warren Lewis, Gervase Mathew, R. B. McCallum, C. E. Stevens, John Wain, Charles Williams, Charles Wrenn, and Christopher Tolkien

1935   Father Francis Morgan dies on June 11

1936   JRRT delivers his seminal lecture on "*Beowulf*: The Monsters and the Critics," to the British Academy; Susan Dagnall, working for publishers Allen & Unwin, reads *The Hobbit* in partial manuscript and persuades JRRT to finish it

1937   *The Hobbit* is published on September 21; JRRT begins work on a sequel at the suggestion of his publisher, Stanley Unwin

1939   World War II begins; Charles Williams moves to Oxford with the wartime relocation of the Oxford University Press and becomes a regular at meetings of the Inklings

1944   Christopher Tolkien is called up for the RAF and posted to South Africa; JRRT sends him drafts of the increasingly unwieldy "new hobbit" manuscript

1945   World War II ends; Tolkien is elected Merton Professor of English Language and Literature at Oxford; Charles Williams dies suddenly

1947   The Tolkiens move to Manor Road

1949   Completion of The Lord of the Rings manuscript; publication of *Farmer Giles of Ham* in the fall

1950   JRRT, displeased with Unwin's treatment of *Farmer Giles* and proposals for cutting The Lord of the Rings, offers his manuscript to Collins Publishers; the Tolkiens move to Holywell Street; the friendship between JRRT and Lewis begins to cool

1952   Collins passes on The Lord of the Rings; Tolkien reapproaches Allen & Unwin

1954   The Tolkiens move to Sandfield Road in Headington, an Oxford suburb; Lewis elected Chair of Medieval and Renaissance Literature at Cambridge; *The Fellowship of the Ring* is published in August; *The Two Towers* follows in November

1955   *The Return of the King* is published in October.

1959   JRRT retires from his professorship at Oxford

1962   *The Adventures of Tom Bombadil* is published; the book was compiled at the suggestion of JRRT's Aunt Jane, who dies shortly after its publication

1963   C. S. Lewis dies on November 22

1964   *Tree and Leaf* is published

1965   Ace Books, an American publisher, brings out an unauthorized paperback edition of *The Lord of the Rings*; the authorized American publishers, Houghton Mifflin, and their paperback arm, Ballantine, rush a paperback into press; the resulting controversy brings the trilogy greater public attention and the Hippie era fascination with Middle-earth begins

1967   *Smith of Wooton Major* is published

1967   The Tolkiens move to Lakeside Road, Poole, near the seaside resort of Bournemouth

1971   Edith Tolkien dies on November 29

1972   JRRT moves back to Oxford, where he is given rooms at Merton College; he is made C.B.E. (Commander of the British Empire) by Queen Elizabeth II in the spring honors list, and receives an honorary Doctorate of Letters from Oxford in June

1973   JRRT receives an honorary doctorate from the University of Edinburgh in June; on a trip to Bournemouth in late August, he is taken ill, and dies on September 2 at the age of eighty-one

Chapter 1

BIRMINGHAM TO BLOEMFONTEIN . . . AND BACK AGAIN (1892–1904)

South Africa in the 1890s was a place where the British sent their super-fluous young men to make something of themselves. For some, especially upper-class youths who had blotted their copybooks with scandalous be-havior back home, it was both a form of exile and an opportunity to in-dulge their excesses far from the censorious eyes of high society. For Arthur Tolkien, the middle-class son of a bankrupt piano manufacturer, it was an opportunity to get a higher-paying management job in his field—bank-ing—than he would have been able to find in England, where competition was sharp and connections, which he lacked, made all the difference.

The Tolkien family had emigrated from Germany to England in the middle of the eighteenth century. Arthur's younger sister Grace claimed that the family was descended from the noble von Hohenzollerns and that the name "Tolkien" (pronounced "toll-keen") was a nickname, originally *tollkühn,* "foolhardy," bestowed on an ancestor who had daringly captured the sultan's standard in a raid against the Turks at the Siege of Vienna in 1529. Whether the Tolkiens had wound up in England by escaping the Prussian invasion of their native Saxony in 1756 or by escaping the guil-lotine in Revolutionary France in 1794, as of the early nineteenth century there were Tolkiens in London, established as makers of clocks, watches, and pianos. John Tolkien moved his business as a piano maker and music seller to Birmingham, in the West Midlands of England, and there he and his wife, Mary, raised their family of three daughters and five sons, the eld-est of whom was Arthur.

Birmingham was one of the main centers of the Industrial Revolution in nineteenth-century England, a hotbed of manufacturing and commerce. Its location is almost exactly the geographic center of England, which led to the city's becoming a focal point of the railway systems that transported its goods to all corners of the country. Economic depressions in the 1870s and 1880s, however, forced many small manufacturers into bankruptcy, including the Tolkiens. In an era when most sons expected to go into the family business, this created an employment vacuum that forced Arthur Tolkien to pursue a career in banking and made immigration to South Africa seem extremely attractive. Newly discovered diamond and gold mines promised ample rewards for a young man willing to travel to, literally, the ends of the earth in order to manage the wealth being pulled out of the ground every day.

Arthur had another incentive to take chances in order to secure a good living: He was engaged to Mabel Suffield, the daughter of yet another bankrupt Birmingham businessman. The Suffields had originally come from the town of Evesham, south of Birmingham and near the border between England and Wales, an area that has been a fertile fruit-growing region since very early times, famous for its apples and pears. The Suffields were Methodists and deeply committed to their church. Mabel and her two sisters had participated in missionary work in Zanzibar, where they attempted to convert the sultan's harem to Christianity, and Mabel had also worked as a governess in England before she was married.

Mabel and Arthur had been unofficially engaged for two years before he left England for South Africa in 1890, and the understanding had been formalized only just before his departure. After a year of hard work and travel, he was named manager of the Lloyd's Bank branch in Bloemfontein, the capital of the Orange Free State (a Dutch, rather than a British, colony). Mabel set sail for Africa in March, and the couple were married immediately upon her arrival in Cape Town on April 16, 1891. Just under nine months later, on January 3, 1892, their elder son, John Ronald Reuel—called Ronald by his family—was born. Two years later he had a baby brother, Hilary Arthur Reuel, born on February 17, 1894.

Arthur Tolkien loved life in South Africa, although the extremes of temperature—blindingly hot in summer, freezing in winter, and dry year-round—did not afford him the best of health. As manager of a British bank branch in a Dutch colony, he had to learn Dutch in order to transact business, and he had to be aggressive in order to attract it. The kind of preexisting social connections that were vital for business in England may not have been as important in South Africa, but making new social connections to create business was a necessity. If a man was to be judged on his own talents, he had to display them prominently. As a result, the elder Tolkien spent much of his time at the office and the club, leaving his wife to tend to the children. He began, in fact, to exhibit all the characteristics of what the late twentieth century would call a workaholic. There was always another project in the works that demanded his attention, for if he did not grab the job, someone else would take the work as well as the glory. If a man wanted to get ahead, his attention could not waver.

As a result, Tolkien's dim adult memories of his South African childhood included few of his father. He claimed to have a strong visual memory of running back to the house in terror after being bitten on the foot by a tarantula when he was two years old, but no memory of the bite itself; he also claimed that this episode had no influence on his portrayals of villainous spiders in both *The Hobbit* and *The Lord of the Rings*.[1] Another story that made it into family lore was the time that the family's houseboy, Isaak, enchanted with the whole concept of white-skinned children, took Ronald to his kraal (or native village), neglecting to inform the family of this unauthorized field trip. Although the family was frantic at Ronald's disappearance, they bore no ill will to Isaak once the truth was understood. Arthur Tolkien spent much of his free time planting trees in the garden under the watchful eyes of his children, attempting to create an English-type grove in this foreign land; this was one of Ronald's strongest memories of his father.

Mabel Tolkien was not as happy with life in South Africa as her husband. She found it too hot and dusty, too far from family and friends, and she was made uncomfortable by the casual racism of colonial life. Although she had had some experience of life in Africa when she did her missionary work in Zanzibar, the circumstances of life in the two countries were hardly comparable; for one thing, Zanzibar was a Muslim country with a much more sophisticated native culture than South Africa and a longer history of both urban life and interaction with European culture; for another thing, Zanzibar, an island, had a much more equable climate than the interior of South Africa. Mabel's homesickness was somewhat alleviated in early 1893 by a visit from her sister and brother-in-law, May and Walter Incledon, who brought their young daughter, Marjorie, with them when Walter had to make a business trip to check on investments in South African mines. Nonetheless, the pleasure of having a sister at hand in whom to confide her dissatisfaction with the pettiness of provincial life only made the contrast all the more painful when the Incledons returned to England. Hopes of early home leave for the entire family were dashed when Mabel became pregnant with Hilary. Even more ominous was Arthur's evident love for the country and his job; it began to appear that even if he had the chance of a permanent job back in England, he might not want to take it. South Africa seemed to offer the opportunities he

wanted and he was uncertain whether he could reacclimate to English society—this despite the fact that the extremes of South Africa's weather
were now compounded by a drought and a plague of locusts. Mabel might
have been forgiven for beginning to feel harassed on a biblical scale.

In April 1895, Mabel and the two boys returned to England without
Arthur. There were several reasons for the decision: The elder Tolkiens
and Suffields had not yet seen their grandsons, and Ronald's health
seemed to suffer from the heat. It was hardly a coincidence that fair-
haired, pale-skinned boys were not native to Africa. The realities of over-
seas employment, however, determined that Arthur Tolkien could not
afford to make the trip with his wife and children, for the terms of his position meant that he would only earn half pay while away from his job;
furthermore, he was unwilling to leave behind pending projects that
would provide more feathers in his cap. The pain of being separated from
his wife and children seemed likely, however, to provide the incentive he
needed to follow them as soon as the pressures of work eased, and he had
every intention of joining them in Birmingham.

Mabel and the boys quickly settled into the routine of life in the
Suffield household, which was somewhat cramped with the addition of
three new bodies, but jovial nonetheless. Ronald's health began to improve and the boys became acquainted with their network of English relatives, a marked change from the general sense of isolation that had made
life in Bloemfontein such a trial for their mother. This happy time was cut
short when news arrived in November that Arthur had contracted rheumatic fever, an inflammatory disease that can cause severe damage to the
heart. Although it is treatable with antibiotics, in the late nineteenth
century there was little recourse for those it struck except for rest in a
warm, dry climate to decrease the spread of the infection. A winter in the
cold and damp of western England was out of the question. Mabel was
preparing to return to South Africa to nurse her husband back to health,
leaving the children in her parents' care, when a telegram arrived to an-
nounce Arthur's death of a hemorrhage on February 15, 1896. Mabel did
not have to return to Africa ever again, but now she was a widow with a
small pension and two children to support.

Tolkien biographer Humphrey Carpenter emphasizes Mabel Tolkien's
strength and determination in taking care of her fatherless children, her
care for their education, and her changing yet deeply held convictions of
faith. To a great extent, this portrait appears to be based on the memories
of her held by Tolkien himself and disseminated through the family. Yet in
the context of late-nineteenth-century England, Mabel appears to have
been an unusual although not unique woman. She was not a stay-at-home

young lady who waited passively for a man to translate her from dependency in her father's house to dependency under her husband's roof; she was part of a new breed of woman who obtained her own education and thought for herself. She was, however, willing to wait for the man she loved, willing to work while she waited for him, and also willing to travel an immense distance, alone, to make a life with him.

Arthur Tolkien appears to have been inspired by the freedom and opportunities of life on a frontier; although in retrospect the legacies of European imperialism in Africa and elsewhere in the world are of contestable value, from the perspective of the imperialists themselves, the far reaches of the earth offered a chance for adventure, wealth, and carving one's own identity rather than being stuck with the class and status of one's family. It may well be that Mabel Tolkien was also inspired by this prospect of freedom, but all too often, the role of women in frontier societies is even more confining than their opportunities in the center of their culture. Women in the "wilderness" are often expected to be the ones who provide a civilizing hand to rein in the excesses of their men. They are expected to recreate an idealized version of "back home" that will balance the rapid changes the men are effecting in the new land. Mabel's dissatisfaction with the pettiness of life in Bloemfontein suggests that she was not content with being the saintly Victorian housewife who provides a refuge from the harsh outside world for her work-weary man, and in fact, she seems to have had a taste for that harsh outside world herself. Certainly she showed no particular predilection for a quiet life at any costs. She made up her mind and followed her heart.

LIFE IN THE SHIRE

The loss of his father marked a major change in Tolkien's life. In addition to the simple lack of a paternal figure, the elder Tolkien had died before he would have been eligible for a pension sufficient to support his family completely, and therefore Mabel and her children were largely dependent upon the Tolkien and Suffield families for financial assistance. Initially, the widow and her sons lived with her parents, where they had already been staying when news of Arthur's death arrived, but relatively soon Mabel was looking for a house of her own. She found a cottage to rent in a small village on the outskirts of Birmingham called Sarehole.

Late-nineteenth-century Birmingham was nicknamed the "Black Country" because of the appalling air pollution created by its factories and mills. Smokestacks were the predominant feature of the skyline. This was the same era when, in London, the combination of industrial air pollutants and the region's severe fogs created smogs that literally killed people—the Industrial Revolution was a dirty business. Yet urban sprawl had not yet completely encompassed the countryside surrounding the big industrial cities; the concept of a "suburb" was just developing and it was still possible to live in a country community within a relatively short distance of the urban center. Sarehole was one of these country oases: a cluster of homes, a mill, a sandpit, a few shops, and several farms about a mile south of the city limits. The locals were country people who worked where they lived, and Mabel and her sons were something of an anomaly, both in being middle class and in being outsiders.

Sarehole was a countryside of meadows, riverbanks, the tantalizingly dangerous works of the sixteenth-century mill, places to pick blackberries or flowers, or mushrooms that were not their own. Tolkien admitted in many of his letters, after *The Lord of the Rings* became a household name, that Sarehole was his model for the Shire, not only in its rural tranquility but also in its aura of a long-lost pastoral Eden.[2] The miller of Sarehole— dubbed the "White Ogre" by the boys—became the paradigm for Ted Sandyman; the old farmer who drove off the boys from stealing his mushrooms—the "Black Ogre"—became Farmer Maggot; and a local inventor, Dr. Gamgee, gave his surname to Samwise and his Gaffer, while his invention—cotton wool—provided the name for the family of Sam's sweetheart, Rosie Cotton.[3] More importantly, this quiet little place provided a retreat where the family could grieve and come to terms with the new parameters of their lives. The trip to Birmingham, after all, originally had been intended as just a visit; now it was a permanence.

Mabel took on the task of teaching her young sons as well. Her previous experience as a governess meant that she was well qualified to do so, but it was also a way to save money. It quickly became evident that Ronald had a particular facility for languages, which was to shape his life in many ways. In some ways, his awareness of language may have been sparked by the number of different kinds of language he had already been exposed to in his short life: the Afrikaans of South Africa, the Zulu-accented English of the family servants, the middle-class Birmingham accents of his parents and their families, and the Warwickshire country accents of the residents of Sarehole, all with their own peculiarities of vocabulary, dialect, and idiom. Even at this early age, it appeared that what attracted Ronald to a language was the sound of it—Latin sounded fascinating to him, French less so. The looks of a word on the page also entranced him, an attraction possibly related to his second facility, that of drawing.

Ronald was reading and learning to write by the age of four; his preferred fare included the cowboy and Indian sagas of the American West, the Arthurian legends, and the fairy stories of George Macdonald. The "ogre" nicknames he and Hilary bestowed on the local characters show that he was also well versed in the dramatis personae of folktales. His favorite books were the fairy-tale collections of Andrew Lang, one of the giants of nineteenth-century folktale scholarship and a guiding light of the Folklore Society. Ironically, given Tolkien's later career as a philologist (a student of words and language), Lang's collections of folktales retold in language suitable for the sensibilities of Victorian children (or perhaps, for the sensibilities of their parents' conceptions of Victorian children) were part of Lang's project for a folklore scholarship based on comparative anthropology, emphasizing folklore as part of a living culture, rather than the philological school of folklore, which valued folklore solely for its accidental preservation of "antiquity." By amassing a treasure trove of folktales from every corner of the world, juxtaposed without regard for their ethnic origins, Lang hoped to awaken in his young readers an interest in the universal themes and motifs of folklore.

It was Lang's *Red Fairy Book* (1890) that struck a spark in Ronald Tolkien's heart with its retelling of the Germanic legend of Sigurd, who slew the dragon Fafnir. This was the stuff from which Richard Wagner had recently constructed his operatic tetralogy *Der Ring des Nibelungen* (1853–1874). Lang's retelling inspired Ronald to write his own dragon story, about a "green great dragon." He later recalled that his mother had corrected his grammar, pointing out that it should be a "great, green dragon," and the question as to why this word order should be preferred to the other stuck in his mind far longer than the plot of the story did.[4] Already, however, the young Tolkien was being exposed to the intimate relationship between the structure of a language and the stories told in it, and as he learned his grammar—English, Latin, or French—he played at narrating with that grammar.

CONVERSION AND ITS CONSEQUENCES

Around the time that Ronald was eight, another major change occurred in his life: In 1900, Mabel Tolkien converted to Catholicism, and her children entered the church with her. In the context of turn-of-the-century Britain, this had much the same impact on, and created much the same reaction in, her family as a college student joining a religious cult in the 1960s. The religious history of Britain is long and complex, but repercussions from Henry VIII's break with the Catholic Church in 1527 were still being felt almost four hundred years later. For one thing, the political turmoil of the sixteenth and seventeenth centuries, when being Catholic or Protestant often also meant that one supported one or another claimant to the British throne, had resulted in laws, not abolished until the nineteenth century, forbidding Catholics from holding positions in government or from being members of Oxford or Cambridge Universities, all of whom were—at least nominally—clergymen in the Anglican Church. (Even in the early twenty-first century, the monarch of Britain cannot marry a Catholic, which has provided the basis for much of the melodrama of Prince Charles's life.) The fact that most English people were Protestant, while most Irish were Catholic, also added an aspect of class distinction to the religious question—Catholicism was the religion of servants, laborers, and political dissidents.

The Anglican Church had by this time settled down to a certain dull emptiness, a social institution rather than a source of faith, its theology more influenced by the intellectual tenets of the Enlightenment than by "enthusiasm," a word that literally refers to a sense that God is within oneself. Groups such as the Baptists, Methodists, Presbyterians, Congregationalists, and Unitarians, as well as the Quakers, Plymouth Brethren, Salvation Army, and others were termed "Nonconformists" for their dissent from mainstream Anglicanism; meanwhile, there were tensions within the Anglican Church between those who favored a more conservative and ritualistic approach to religions (termed "High Church" Anglicans) and those who saw the church as more of a force for social reform and personal spirituality ("Low Church" Evangelicals). Most Nonconformist religions had begun as Low Church movements within the Anglican Church. High Church Anglicanism, for its part, could come very close to being simply Catholicism without the Pope—Henry VIII had not been particularly interested in changing his spiritual beliefs when he broke with Rome; he simply wanted the political freedom to divorce his wife, Catherine of Aragon, and marry Anne Boleyn.

Mabel's journey to Catholic conversion had begun with a slow drift from Low Church to High, until finally even High Church Anglicanism was not enough for her. Birmingham was the home of one of the most famous English Catholic converts of the nineteenth century, John Henry (later Cardinal) Newman. He, too, had begun as an Evangelical Anglican and had moved slowly but progressively to High. During his time as an Oxford don (the term referring to a teacher—a tutor, fellow, or professor—at Oxford or Cambridge University), he had been one of the leading lights of the Oxford Movement, which preached that "the Church was not established by the State. It was sanctified because the Church was a holy body descended from the twelve Apostles." [5] After leaving Oxford, Newman had established an oratory of the Order of St. Philip Neri in Birmingham. Here a community of priests and lay brothers conducted services and taught in a Catholic school. Although this was not the church Mabel and her sons initially attended, it was the one to which they eventually gravitated.

Mabel Tolkien's family were Nonconformists. Her father was a Unitarian, and most of the rest of her family were Methodists. Her sister May—who converted to Catholicism along with Mabel—was married to an Anglican who laid great store by his social position in the local Anglican church. The Tolkiens, for their part, were mostly Baptists. As historian Walter L. Arnstein notes, by the middle of the nineteenth century,

> The faithful evangelical looked upon such Roman Catholic institutions as the priesthood (a celibate caste wielding miraculous powers), the mass (a reenactment of Christ's original sacrifice), and the papacy (an institution with supreme spiritual jurisdiction over all Christians) as theologically erroneous and morally repugnant ... . Closely tied to the revived sense of repugnance toward Rome's theological tenets was a revival of the historical fears of a divided loyalty among English Roman Catholics and a renewed concern with the immoral practices that, in Protestant eyes, seemed all too likely to result from clerical celibacy, the seclusion of young women in convents, and the secrecy of confessional. The priest was viewed as a rival father likely to disrupt the domestic unity of the patriarchal Victorian family.[6]

Since she was a widow, Mabel Tolkien's conversion to Catholicism was not about to undermine her husband's patriarchal authority; however, her defiance of the wishes of both her own family and her in-laws meant that her financial position became even more dire than before. Moreover, her sons were now of an age where she could no longer teach them. If they were to make anything of themselves in life, they needed to go to a proper school, and a good one at that.

Arthur Tolkien had been a student at King Edward's School, the oldest school in Birmingham. It was not as prestigious as Eton, Harrow, and Rugby, but it still managed to send a few students every year to Oxford and Cambridge. The school was founded in 1552 under the auspices of Edward VI, although its antecedents probably went back to the reign of Richard II (king from 1377–1399), when four Birmingham men endowed a charity for education. A Victorian Gothic building had been erected in 1833 to house the school, designed by Charles Barry, the architect of the newly rebuilt Houses of Parliament. Ronald took a scholarship examination in 1899, when he was seven, but failed to be admitted. However, he was able to pass the exam the next year, and so in 1900 he began his formal academic career.

It was a long trek for a small boy into Birmingham every day, and so Mabel moved the family back to the main part of town. She could not afford anywhere as nice as the house in Sarehole, however, and the first place they lived turned out to be a condemned property. The second house backed onto the railway tracks leading into and out of King's Heath Station, which was on the line from Birmingham into Wales, and it was here that Ronald had his first exposure to the mysteries of the Welsh language in the incomprehensible spellings of the names on the sides of the trains that ran past their back windows. What kind of word was "Penrhiwceiber"? The distribution of vowels and consonants makes no sense to an English speaker. "Senghenydd"? "Nantyglo"? Up to this time, he had only been exposed to languages descended from the Germanic and Latin families of Europe, and Ronald's native Modern English has a vocabulary that derives from both sides of the family—the words he learned in Latin or French had cognates in English and were not inescapably foreign to his linguistic sensibilities. Welsh, a Celtic language, has a very different word stock, and the music of its possible sounds opened new possibilities to a boy with an innate taste for language.

Finally, Mabel discovered the Birmingham Oratory, which not only appealed to her religious sensibilities but also owned a small house that was for rent. The Tolkiens moved in, the boys were enrolled in the Catholic school next door, and at first the arrangement seemed to solve all of the family's problems. However, the quality of teaching at the Oratory school was not as acceptable as the quality of its religious services, at least not for a student of Ronald's academic bent (Hilary was much less of a scholar). By the 1903 school year, Ronald was back at King Edward's, this time on a scholarship that paid all his fees, so that Mabel was not dependent on family goodwill to assure his education.

While church was of increasing importance in the Tolkien family life, the Birmingham Oratory's longest-lasting effect on Ronald Tolkien was to introduce the family to Father Francis Morgan, one of the Oratory's priests. Father Morgan—half Welsh and half Anglo-Spanish, with a personal income derived from his family's sherry importing business—took the Tolkiens under his wing, offering Mabel the advice and emotional support she was so sadly lacking from most of her own family. Father Morgan was a loud, kind, jolly man, whose emotional extravagance was often attributed to his Spanish blood. He was, by all accounts, a man who interacted with the world through his heart rather than his head. In acknowledgment of this friendship, Mabel named him, rather than any of her or her late husband's relatives, the guardian of the two boys, should anything happen to her.

This may have been a prescient move, for Mabel's health began to decline. In April 1904, she was hospitalized, and it was discovered that she had diabetes. Once again, Ronald was taken out of school and sent to live with his mother's sister Jane and her husband in Hove, near Brighton, while Hilary went to stay with Mabel's parents. At this time, before the discovery of the role of insulin in managing diabetes, and long before the pharmaceutical production of insulin for the use of diabetics, there was little to do to manage the disease. Modification of diet might be prescribed—some diabetics were advised to become vegetarian, for instance—but the side effects of the disease sooner or later brought death. In later years, Tolkien blamed his mother's ill health on the stress of living the life of an impoverished widow and held her family accountable for not doing more to ease her difficulties. Indeed, recent research into adult-onset diabetes has shown that consistent emotional stress plays a great part in destroying the body's ability to manufacture and use its own insulin, so Tolkien was not too far off in his intuitive diagnosis. The effect on his own life, however, was to impress on his mind that his mother was being punished for her conversion to Catholicism, and that it was his duty to stick to the faith that she had chosen out of loyalty to her memory— the rest of her family might have abandoned her, but he never would. The idea of "the Mother Church" had a very literal resonance for him.

Mabel recovered enough to leave the hospital, and Father Morgan arranged for the family to spend the summer in a cottage located on the grounds of a country house owned by the Oratory in Rednal outside Birmingham. It was one last return to the idyllic country life that they had left behind in Sarehole. Yet every summer comes to an end, and the beginning of the school year saw the family back in Birmingham, and Ronald back at King Edward's. However, on November 8, 1904, Mabel slipped into a diabetic coma, and died six days later.

NOTES

1. Humphrey Carpenter, *The Letters of J. R. R. Tolkien* (Boston: Houghton Mifflin, 2000), 217.

2. Carpenter, *Letters,* 230, 235, 390.

3. Carpenter, *J. R. R. Tolkien: A Biography* (Boston: Houghton Mifflin, 1977), 28–29.

4. Carpenter, *Letters*, 214.

5. Noel Annan, *The Dons: Mentors, Eccentrics, and Geniuses* (Chicago: University of Chicago Press, 1999), 48.

6. Walter L. Arnstein, *Protestant versus Catholic in Mid-Victorian England: Mr. Newdegate and the Nuns* (Columbia: University of Missouri Press, 1982), 3–4.

Chapter 2

GRAMMARS AND A GIRL
(1904–1910)

Tolkien was twelve years old when his mother died. His life to this point had been insecure and unsettled, as the family had moved from house to house in and out of Birmingham, and Ronald and Hilary flitted into, out of, and between schools. In addition to the constant physical dislocation, the emotional uncertainty caused by family members who initially loved, but then abhorred them based solely (it must have seemed) on which church they attended can only have aroused psychological insecurities in the boys. The only consistent factor in their lives had been their mother, and now she, too, was gone. The two periods of relative peace and happiness, at least in Tolkien's adult memories, were the years at Sarehole and the brief summer at Rednal, the latter apparently a kind of recap of the earlier idyll, which Tolkien appreciated all the more for having in the interim experienced all the privations that near-poverty-level life in a turn-of-the-century industrial city had to offer. In a letter to one of his grandsons, more than sixty years after Mabel's death, Tolkien still seemed bitter about her sufferings and still associated her death with loyalty to the Catholic church, using terms highly suggestive of the kind of martyrdom suffered by the early saints who turned their backs on lives of comfort and lived in poverty as a testament to their faith.[1]

The other place that Tolkien experienced returning to was King Edward's School. It had been hard to maintain his studies, first in the bare bones academic atmosphere of St. Philip's and then on his own, living with his aunt's family near Brighton when his mother first became ill. It was also hard to maintain friendships when his attendance record was so erratic. It had been clear from the time Mabel had first started home-schooling the boys that Ronald was the brainy one, with a natural linguistic bent. His preteen education, however, had been so erratic that it is unlikely that he had ever really applied himself to any academic endeavor that did not already appeal to him. While he seemed to have the potential for achieving a place at Oxford or Cambridge, he would be the first in his family to attend university, and as such, was something of an odd duck.

BRITISH EDUCATION

The type of education that schools such as King Edward's offered at the turn of the twentieth century was very different from the state-sponsored education provided in Europe and America at the turn of the twenty-first. Public school education—that is, what in the United States would be called private school—was originally based on the assumption that all a gentleman needed to do to be well educated was to have a thorough grounding in Latin and Greek. One learned the grammar, read a small but significant list of classic writers, and composed both prose and verse in their imitation. Since many of these authors were historians and geographers as well as literary writers, the topics of ancient history and geography were considered suitable for study as well, and the study of mathematics and of French—the language of sophistication that would allow the gentleman to converse with his Continental counterparts should the occasion arise—were also acceptable. Music, drawing, fencing, dancing, and military exercises were "extras."[2]

Prior to the nineteenth century, public schools were intended to educate the gentry, and although many of the young men who attended them might also move on to Oxford or Cambridge, neither the public school nor, necessarily, the universities were intended to foster much in the way of intellectual achievement. The men they produced did not have to worry about obtaining gainful employment; they would run the family estates, buy a commission in the army or navy and police or govern the ever-enlarging British Empire, stand for Parliament if they were not already entitled to sit in the House of Lords, enter the Anglican clergy and obtain a "living"—a parish—often through family connections, or, if all else failed, marry an heiress. The very idea of a "job" or even a "career" was relatively new. One did what one's family did—ruled the land, cultivated it, or made things from its products. One did these things on a timetable dictated by the seasons and the amount of daylight available at any given time in the year's round. The Industrial Revolution introduced the idea of going to a specific job, where one worked a set number of hours and produced goods by means of machine work, but the people who did these jobs were lower class, not at all the type of person who attended school of any sort. The idea of choosing a job because one was interested in it was almost unheard of. The local economy or family tradition dictated one's occupation.

The education offered in the public schools and universities produced men who were trained to talk to each other on the same level and to influence each other through words. Everyone had read roughly the same books, everyone had been taught to write in a similar mode, everyone had the same general conception of the world, its history and shape; what tactics had worked in wars over the ages; how to add, subtract, multiply, and divide sufficiently for daily use; and some acquaintance with the cultural equipment that made a man a genial companion in social situations. Science was an esoteric subject that men took up as a hobby; if intellectual curiosity inspired them to invent or discover something, that was just gravy. Intellectual curiosity was purely a matter of personal choice, and frankly, a choice best exercised, and funded, in private.

Throughout the nineteenth century, especially as the populations of urban centers exploded, the idea arose that everyone should have some kind of formal education. In part, this was because the kind of informal education that the lower classes had previously received, which was oriented towards understanding the workings of the world from an agricultural or handcrafting perspective, was being lost, and all anyone was learning was how to run machines. The nineteenth century saw the evolution of the idea that the government should provide at least a minimal level of education to all children regardless of family income, and also that those children who were intellectually gifted should have the opportunity to attend university. However, as a result of the religious turmoil that had marked Britain in the sixteenth and seventeenth centuries, matriculation at Oxford and Cambridge was contingent upon swearing to uphold, if not actively participate in, the Anglican Church. It was not until the middle of the nineteenth century that Parliament passed legislation opening the universities to Nonconformists. At the same time, the notion was arising that a university was not merely a breeding ground for clergymen and a finishing school for gentlemen, but should train men in what John Newman—the same John Newman who founded the Birmingham Oratory—called, in his *Idea of the University* (1852), "habits of accurate, thorough, and systematic thinking."[3]

The elder Tolkiens and Suffields would have been of the generation and class that acquired the Three R's in their formal schooling when young but entered the working world by their teen years and learned on the job what was needed for the job. By the end of the nineteenth century, a new middle class had emerged that needed a solid grounding in practical education as it applied to business and manufacturing, but also desired for its sons at least some of the trappings of the classic public school education in order to participate in "culture." Tolkien's father, Arthur, would have been one of these men, attending King Edward's School, with its basically public school ethos, but then going into banking, where being able to "talk the talk" of the upper classes would be a business asset. Tolkien, in turn, never seems to have considered any career other than an academic one. For him, learning was an end in and of itself, undertaken because he was so self-evidently good at it. Throughout his life, although he was bitterly aware of financial hardships and anxious to improve his bank balance, Tolkien never seems to have considered any way of earning money outside of the traditional academic skills of teaching and writing. (His equally unworldly but unintellectual brother, Hilary, in contrast, became a small-time farmer.)

One reason that Tolkien may have stuck to the academic path was that school offered him a source of stability in his life. However, in spite of the fact that Tolkien ultimately became an academic, several aspects of his school days did not fit the academic stereotype. He was an avid rugby player, once biting his tongue so badly during a game that he could blame the mishap well into old age for his indistinct enunciation, even though most of his friends and family were well aware that he just plain mumbled. Despite his unclear speaking, he was also an amateur actor and a member of the debating society—using skills that later made him a popular lecturer, renowned for his dramatic recitations of Old English verse. He formed many friendships and was all in all a very social being. Somehow, although many people commented on how difficult it was to understand exactly what he was saying, he was a persuasive and charismatic performer.

THE BIRTH OF A PHILOLOGIST

Tolkien was enamored of language to a degree far beyond the youthful facility for picking up language that every human has before puberty—not only had he enjoyed learning Latin and, to a lesser extent, French from his mother, but in his idyllic childhood days he and his cousins, Marjorie and Mary Incledon, had invented their own "languages," really codes in which one nonsense word stood for another word in English. These languages seem still to have conformed to the grammar of English, however, so the invention was really in vocabulary rather than in the language as a whole. The point of childhood languages, however, is to be secret, to have a way of communicating without the adults knowing what is being said. While Tolkien excelled at languages in his schooling, he seems never to have lost that childish love of an invented language as a private communication.

Tolkien was lucky that he had several teachers at King Edward's who recognized and encouraged his linguistic abilities. George Brewerton, who taught Tolkien when he first returned after the failed St. Philip's experiment, was a fervent medievalist with a fondness for words of Anglo-Saxon rather than French origin. This may well have been when Tolkien first became aware of the schizophrenic nature of the English language.

English is ultimately a Germanic language, descended from the languages spoken by the Angles, Saxons, and Jutes who began to settle and/or invade Britain in the fifth and sixth centuries. When the Normans, led by William the Conqueror, invaded England in 1066, they imposed their medieval French language (descended from the Latin spoken when France was a province of the Roman Empire) on the government of Britain. For approximately four centuries there were two languages spoken in England, the Norman French of the upper classes and the Anglo-Saxon of the lower classes. (The situation was more complex in the Celtic-speaking areas of Britain, Wales, Cornwall, and Scotland, where three languages competed.) In addition, Latin was the language of the church. Eventually, however, Norman French and Anglo-Saxon merged to become English, a language with a basically Germanic grammar that retained the vocabulary of both Anglo-Saxon and French. "Talk," for instance, is a Germanic word while "conversation" comes from French; likewise "man" versus "person," or "womanly" versus "female." These words tended to retain the cultural values of the people who had originally spoken them, so that Anglo-Saxon-derived words are still generally considered to be vulgar or at least more explicit and direct, while French-derived words are more intellectual but also more euphemistic; a classic example of this cultural divide is the fact that a major meat source is called by the Germanic word "cow" when it is still on the hoof and being tended by a peasant, but is transformed into French "beef" when it has made its way to the nobleman's table. George Brewerton was known for insisting that boys use the Anglo-Saxon word "muck" instead of the French-derived "manure."[4]

The first great writer of the newly synthesized English language, known now as Middle English, is considered to be Geoffrey Chaucer, the author of the *Canterbury Tales*, who lived circa 1342 to 1400. Brewerton encouraged his students to read the *Canterbury Tales* in translation—a collection that ranges from the romantically chivalrous to the earthily bawdy—and recited the original Middle English in class. The languages Tolkien had learned up to this time were presented as being consistent over time—a speaker of Modern English can read Shakespeare, perhaps with some difficulty, but Shakespeare's English is still recognizable as "antiquated" English. The Latin that schoolboys learned was classical Latin, a language that was spoken and understood throughout the Roman Empire. Middle English was the first language Tolkien encountered that was recognizably ancestral to what is spoken today, but largely incomprehensible unless studied as a "foreign" tongue. The idea of a history of language was presented to him for the first time, and it was an idea he wanted to pursue. This is the study of philology.

As Tolkien passed through his classes, his interest in languages was noted by his teachers. By the time he was sixteen, his classics teacher, Robert Cary Gilson—who was also the headmaster of the school—was encouraging young Tolkien not only to learn to translate Greek and Latin but also to investigate the structure of the languages and to proceed from there to the study of general linguistics. George Brewerton, meanwhile, gave him a primer of Anglo-Saxon, the language that preceded Middle English and was spoken from roughly 600–1100 C.E. With the help of the book's explanations of grammar and syntax, Tolkien taught himself to translate the language.

Learning a "dead" language—one that is no longer spoken—is a different matter than learning a language that is still alive. In the case of a live language, the emphasis is on learning to speak, to communicate in conversation, and to understand the words as they are heard from the lips of another speaker. A living language is in a constant state of evolution, with new words being introduced and older words dropping out; there is also a difference between the formal language, such as is used in schools, business, or government, and the idiomatic language spoken on the street. Furthermore, if you come across a word you do not understand, you can always track down a native speaker and just ask. Dead languages are limited by a number of factors. First of all, the only words that are preserved are the ones that were written down. There is little guide to pronunciation, although here poetry can be useful, for words that are obviously intended to rhyme must be pronounced similarly. The longer the language has been dead, the fewer manuscripts or inscriptions are likely to have survived; therefore, a word may only appear once in the entire available body of text, and if the meaning is not clear from the context, guesswork is involved in figuring it out. Verb forms are also limited by manuscript survival: The complete declension of a verb may not be attested, and therefore it is necessary to fill in the blanks, again based on comparison with other words that have survived more fully and on overall patterns within the language family.

Most important, the only way to learn a dead language is to read it, and this is limited by what has survived to be read. In the ages before the invention of paper and printing, manuscripts were written by hand, usually on vellum, which is a material made out of animal hide that requires a great deal of preparation to make ready for the ink. Things were only written down if they were so important that they were worth the cost in time and money to create a manuscript. Since literacy was brought to northern Europe by Christianity, the church held a monopoly on writing for a long time, using it to preserve religious texts and monastery records, often land deeds and monetary accounts. However, aside from the Bible, it is interesting that most of the earliest narrative preserved in writing in Europe is heroic epic and poetry—the tales of heroes, and sometimes of pagan gods disguised as heroes—that predate the arrival of Christianity.

As Tolkien learned to read Anglo-Saxon, then, he soon encountered the major epic poem of that language, *Beowulf*. The original poem exists in only one manuscript, written around 1000 C.E., and tells the story of a sixth-century hero of the Danes who defeats three monsters: first, as a young warrior, the man-eater Grendel, who has been ravaging the court of King Hrothgar, and then Grendel's mother, who attempts to avenge her son; and in his old age, a dragon who seeks to avenge the theft of his treasure-hoard. This last battle proves fatal for Beowulf as well. *Beowulf* is a tough poem, a story of a warrior among cowards, an honest man among thieves, peaceful kings in the midst of feuds, and of a society in which life is nasty, brutish, and short even without the interference of ghoulish monsters and vengeful dragons. It is also a poem that is not particularly notable for its love interest—an aspect that probably later influenced the male-dominated casts of characters in Tolkien's own fiction. The only two female characters of any note are Hrothgar's queen, a largely ceremonial role, and Grendel's mother, who out-monsters her son. But it is a story with a dragon, who may not have been green or great but was a dragon nonetheless. Tolkien was not only encountering the roots of his language, but also the roots of the fairy stories that so enchanted him in the halcyon days when his mother was alive and his only teacher.

THE TEA CLUB, BARROVIAN SOCIETY

Now that Tolkien was attending King Edward's regularly and uninterruptedly, he also began to make lasting friendships with other boys. Christopher Wiseman was one of the first, a boy a year older than he but in the same class; the two were rivals for the position of best student and found that despite differences of opinion in religious matters (Wiseman was a Methodist), they could, and would, talk about anything. Another was Robert Quilter (R.Q.) Gilson, the headmaster's son. Wiseman's bent was towards mathematics, the natural sciences, and music, while Gilson's was towards drawing and design, especially the art of the Renaissance and the eighteenth century. Later, the threesome was augmented by Geoffrey Bache (G.B.) Smith, whose fondness for modern literature, and especially poetry, complemented Tolkien's expertise in the ancient literatures and languages. Under Smith's influence, this quartet began to make their first steps in the composition of poetry—a time-honored adolescent pastime, especially in those days when poets were revered as the creative artists par excellence, and a talented person might even earn a living at it.

A number of the senior students at King Edward's were given responsibility for running the library, under the somewhat lax eye of an assistant schoolmaster. Tolkien, Wiseman, and Gilson entered this inner circle in 1911, along with a few other boys, and soon had instituted a covert ongoing tea party by sneaking in refreshments, a tea kettle, and a spirit-lamp on which to boil the water. This group began to call itself the Tea Club, or "T.C." As time went on, they began meeting as well in the tearoom of a Birmingham department store called Barrow's Stores, where there was a table set up in a little alcove known as the "Railway Carriage" that seated the group cozily. Wiseman expanded the name to "T.C.B.S.," the "Tea Club, Barrovian Society." Although the exact membership fluctuated, Tolkien, Wiseman, Gilson, and Smith retained the moniker for themselves even after they had left school and moved on to university.

The group existed mostly to talk and snack. As boys who spent most of their lives in school, who were expected (and who themselves expected) to go on to university, whose emotional currency, so to speak, was academics, they tended to talk about the things they were studying. They were all boys who were fired by intellectual and artistic discovery; Tolkien and Wiseman, for instance, may have shared a love of playing rugby, but their real competition was with their brains. Since their interests were so diverse, however, it was largely a matter of each sharing the new knowledge that fired his own imagination. Tolkien regaled them with tales from medieval myth and epic, gruesome tales of slaughter and vengeance from the Norse *Volsüngasaga* or the Middle English poem of *Sir Gawain and the Green Knight* (which includes the slightly disconcerting episode of a man who not only has his head cut off, but then picks it up and walks out of the court with it tucked under his arm, talking).

HOME LIFE AND LOVE

Yet while one half of Tolkien's world was the chummy schoolboy life of a typical, if markedly intelligent, middle-class English boy in the first decade of the twentieth century, the other half was somewhat more unconventional. Mabel Tolkien had named Father Francis Morgan the guardian of her boys, but since he was a priest who lived at the Birmingham Oratory, he did not have a home in which to raise them. His guardianship was somewhat less hands-on than literally raising Ronald and Hilary himself, as their relatives would have done if Mabel had named one of her or Arthur's siblings as a guardian. Religion was a touchy question; Mabel had named Father Morgan as guardian specifically because she did not want relatives to reconvert the boys back to some version of Protestantism.

Since living at the Birmingham Oratory was not possible, Father Morgan had to find some place for Ronald and Hilary to board. The first solution was to have them live in Birmingham with their Aunt Beatrice, the widow of Mabel's brother William, who had also died in 1904. Beatrice was one of the few Suffield relatives who did not have any interest in the boys' religion and did not interfere with Father Morgan's continuing care of their spiritual life. Her finances were as slender as Mabel's had been, and she was simply glad to get the money for the boys' room and board. However, as a new widow herself, she had her own grieving to take care of and was not in a state to offer much consolation to two recently orphaned boys. The house was dreary, with no view from the windows save the rooftops of houses in the neighborhood. The countryside where the boys had lived with Mabel seemed increasingly lost to the past. Other aspects of the past were lost as well—Beatrice burned all of Mabel's letters one day, presumably because she considered them to be just clutter taking up space, without considering that Mabel's sons might like to keep some memories of their mother.

The boys were soon merely sleeping and eating at Beatrice's house, spending the rest of the day either at school or at the Oratory with Father Morgan. In addition, they would spend their summer vacations at the seaside at Lyme Regis with Father Morgan, walking and sketching and talking. Eventually, Father Morgan realized that the depression that afflicted the two boys was more than merely grieving for their mother—they were seriously unhappy living with Beatrice Suffield. He looked for another boarding establishment that would take in two teenaged orphans, and in 1908, Ronald and Hilary moved to the house of a Mrs. Faulkener, who lived near the Oratory on Duchess Road. The household also included Mrs. Faulkener's wine-merchant husband and the couple's daughter, as well as another orphaned lodger, a young woman named Edith Bratt, three years older than Ronald and five years older than Hilary.

Edith was the illegitimate daughter of Frances Bratt, whose family were boot and shoe manufacturers in Wolverhampton. Her mother was thirty—an age when women were usually considered unmarriageable in this era—when Edith was born, and she never married, raising her daughter alone with the help of a cousin, Jennie Grove. Despite the stigma of illegitimacy, Edith's life was reasonably happy until her mother died when Edith was fourteen. There was enough money for her to have a secure home; her natural talent as a pianist was encouraged and she was sent to a boarding school that specialized in music education after her mother's death. She inherited enough money to keep her comfortably as a lodger in someone else's house, though perhaps not enough to set up house on her own. It was expected that she would become a piano teacher or even a concert pianist; the rationale for her lodging with Mrs. Faulkener after leaving school was that the landlady had a reputation for her "musical" parties and it was assumed that the environment would further encourage Edith's talents. However, it seemed that Mrs. Faulkener was fond of hearing music performed but did not have the patience to hear someone practicing scales in the parlor for extended periods of time. At the time that the Tolkien boys entered the Faulkener ménage, Edith was at something of a loose end, spending most of her time working on her sewing machine in her own room.

Ronald and Hilary shared a room on the second floor, directly above Edith's. The three soon found themselves spending much of their time at home together; in particular, they conspired with the maid to hoist extra food up into their rooms by means of a basket on the end of a rope. It was an alliance of outsiders against the "Old Lady," as they called Mrs. Faulkener. Ronald and Edith also began frequenting teashops together. Ronald did not have very much experience with young women of his own age. The women in his life had up to this point all been of his mother's generation, or his cousins Mary and Marjorie Incledon (whom he did not see very often after the Catholic conversion). His school life was strictly male, his guardian was a member of and lived in an all-male institution, and his only surviving nuclear family member was a brother. His school friendships, especially the T.C.B.S., were close ones, but their focus was on the sharing of intellectual excitements. Although the T.C.B.S. seems to have partaken of the ideal of a noble closeness of like-minded males that prevailed in the late-nineteenth and early-twentieth centuries, this kind of male friendship tended to bind boys and men in a devotion to ideals such as art or literature (as with Tolkien and his friends), or religion, the military, or some other institution. Although little documentation remains of what Ronald and Edith shared in these early years of their lives, after her death Tolkien made reference to "the dreadful sufferings of our childhoods, from which we rescued one another," adding that they "could not wholly heal the wounds that later often proved disabling."[5] This suggests that what the two shared was purely emotional rather than intellectual, the flip side of Tolkien's school friendships. It also suggests that Edith was the one person to whom Tolkien truly opened up about his feelings about the loss of his parents and the estrangement from his parents' families. At the same time, his life with Edith was completely compartmentalized from his school life, and none of his friends realized that Tolkien was also involved in what was slowly turning into a romance.

The budding love affair between Ronald and Edith soon turned into something almost approaching a 1920s romantic comedy: young lovers separated by a guardian's ban, secret meetings uncovered by accident, defiance, misunderstandings, and (eventually) a happy ending. It was 1909: Tolkien was supposed to be preparing for his entrance exams for Oxford in the fall, and attendance at the university was contingent upon his gaining a scholarship. However, gossip reached Father Morgan's ears that young Ronald was spending more time with a young lady in the teashops of Birmingham than in hitting the books. (One cannot help but wonder at Tolkien's diet during this period—he seems to have spent the greater part of his waking hours having tea with someone or other, whether the T.C.B.S. or Edith.) The fact that Ronald and Edith lived in the same house made the potential for scandal even greater. Father Morgan demanded that Ronald break off the relationship and quickly arranged for new lodgings for the Tolkien boys to get Ronald out of Edith's orbit. In the midst of all of the brouhaha, the time came for Tolkien to take his scholarship exam, and he failed. This was actually not so unusual an occurrence and there was every reason to believe he would pass the next year, but in the face of Father Morgan's accusations that Edith was distracting him from his studies, on which his entire future depended, failure no doubt seemed to prove his guardian right.

Although Father Morgan had forbidden a romantic entanglement between Ronald and Edith, he had neglected to specifically forbid them from seeing each other. They met on several occasions in the early months of 1910, discussing plans. Edith had been invited to live in Cheltenham, a genteel resort town south of Birmingham, in Gloucestershire, with friends named the Jessops, and she had a school friend named Molly Field who lived nearby. To Ronald and Edith, it seemed a good idea for her to take up this offer to defuse the situation, although it was not possible for her to move immediately. Unfortunately, the couple was spotted again in a teashop, and this time Father Morgan insisted that Ronald specifically not see Edith except to say good-bye on the day she left Birmingham; after that, Ronald was not to communicate with her in any way until he turned twenty-one and was no longer under Father Morgan's guardianship.

However, the Tolkiens were still lodging in the vicinity of the Birmingham Oratory, which was the reason for the selection of Mrs. Faulkener's house as a home for the boys in the first place, and Edith was still living at Mrs. Faulkener's. Living in virtually the same neighborhood, Ronald and Edith could hardly help but run into each other by accident on occasion, and it seemed that each accidental meeting made its way to Father Morgan's ears, until he finally forbade even a parting meeting for the two. On the day Edith took the train from Birmingham, Tolkien had no choice but to simply lurk in the streets in hopes of catching one last glimpse. At first it seemed that he would be out of luck, but finally he saw her riding her bicycle to the train station before she left his life for the three years until his twenty-first birthday; at the time, for all he knew, she was leaving his life forever.

NOTES

1. Carpenter, *Letters*, 353–54.

2. Ward, A. W., and W. P. Trent, et al., eds., *The Cambridge History of English and American Literature in Eighteen Volumes*. Volume 14, *The Victorian Age* (New York: G. P. Putnam's Sons, 1907–1921), 12.

3. Ibid., p. 54.

4. Carpenter, *Biography*, 35–36.

5. Carpenter, *Letters*, 421.

Chapter 3

OXFORD (1911–1914)

If nothing else, Edith Bratt's departure from Birmingham gave Ronald no excuse to do anything but study for his Oxford entrance exams, and on the second try, he passed. Given his rather dire finances, he could not afford to attend the university unless he received some kind of financial aid. The nineteenth century had seen much agitation for reform at the two premier universities of Oxford and Cambridge, especially to ameliorate the exclusively wealthy, upper-class character of the undergraduate body. The universities had been charged to award scholarships solely on academic merit rather than on personal connections and to increase the amount of financial assistance available to less wealthy students. There were at the time two forms of aid available, scholarships and exhibitions. The applicant took one test to qualify for either; the scholarships were awarded purely on exam performance, while the exhibitions, which provided somewhat less money, used the exam to identify academically promising but financially needy applicants. (The amount awarded for a scholarship would cover nearly all of a student's expenses for an academic year, while an exhibition would cover most of the expenses but would still require supplementation from the student's own resources.) An applicant taking the exam had to name, in order of preference, the colleges he wished to attend, and once the results were in, the colleges decided which of the applicants who were interested in them they wished to take. Tolkien won an exhibition to Exeter College, one of the less expensive colleges, and Father Morgan was willing to help him out with the extra expenses not covered by the exhibition.

COLLEGE LIFE

For the first two years, students generally lived in rooms at their college. Rooms—a sitting room/study and a bedroom—were located off of staircases, and a servant, or "scout," attended all the rooms on one staircase. A handbook for the university, although written two decades after Tolkien's own student days, makes comments about undergraduate accommodations that probably apply to his time as well:

> The new arrival is told on which staircase his rooms are found, and, unless he is captious, he will be well-satisfied with his sitting-room, which is usually a comfortable and reasonably commodious place, though by no means luxurious. If he is fastidious, he may be a little critical of his bedroom, which is generally of the proportions of a cubicle, and severely inornate. But builders of old evidently believed that in a place to which one resorts in order to become unconscious of one's surroundings, the surroundings do not greatly matter; and the occupant, after one look at the floral luxuriance of the wallpaper, will probably appreciate the advantages of unconsciousness.[1]

The scout brought his students breakfast and often lunch in their rooms; tea was available in the Junior Common Room (a sort of student lounge) or brewed in one's own room; and dinner, the one formal meal of the day, was served to both dons and students in the college's Hall. The fellows of the college—the teaching faculty—sat at High Table (set across the top of the Hall), while the students sat below at a table (or tables) perpendicular to the High Table, an arrangement directly descended from the seating arrangements of medieval banqueting halls.

The academic year was divided into three eight-week terms with substantial vacations in between. Michaelmas Term began in mid-October and ran to early December, followed by a six-week vacation. Hilary Term (also called Lent Term) ran from mid-January to mid-March, again followed by a six-week vacation. Summer Term (also called Trinity Term) ran from late April to late June, and was followed by the Long Vacation, approximately four months long. The amount of "vacation" time should not be misconstrued, however. Students were expected to do most of their reading for the upcoming term during the vacation beforehand. Tutors and other senior academics often organized "reading parties" or trips abroad during vacations, when smaller groups of undergraduates would work together informally. C. S. Lewis gave one of his students the following advice in 1931, explaining the purpose of vacations and the way one should "read" one's subject: "As regards reading for the Vac. [i.e., the Long Vacation], my general view is that the Vac. should be given chiefly to reading the actual literary texts, without much attention to problems, getting thoroughly familiar with stories, situation, and style, and so having all the data for *aesthetic* judgment ready; then the term can be kept for more scholarly reading."[2]

A student entered Oxford with a good idea of what he wanted to major in (as Americans would say) or "read" (as the British say). Often he applied to a college because he specifically wished to study with one of the fellows there. After passing the entrance exam (called "responsions"), the student, accepted by a college within the university, had to matriculate, or enter his name in the official rolls of the university. In order to gain his degree, a student had to be in residence for nine terms—three academic years—although the terms did not have to be consecutive. If he wished to take an honors degree, he was generally in residence for four years. On his arrival at the university he was assigned to a tutor, who oversaw his course of education by compiling a reading list that would prepare the student for his exams, suggest lectures that he should attend, and meet with him—usually weekly—to discuss his reading and assess his progress. If the student was engaged in language study, he would probably meet with his tutor alone and work through translations of classic works; if the study was more amenable to essay-writing, the tutor would often have several students meet with him at once, each taking turns to write an essay that he would present to the group—and the tutor—for critique. Yet, while there were exams at the year's end that assessed students' progress, these exams were based on what a student should, in general, know by this point. The concept of teaching a specific class—say, Greek history—and then setting an examination based only on what had been taught in that class was completely foreign to the Oxford system. Undergraduates were expected to be reading the original texts in their chosen fields—Plato himself, not a translation of Plato, not a book about Platonic philosophy—and then to be able to answer any question on the general topic of Plato and his writings, whether or not it had been discussed with their tutor or raised by their lecturer. "Is this going to be on the final?" was a completely meaningless question. Often, the person writing the exam and/or the person grading it was not even the person who had taught the class.

Tolkien intended to read Greats, the common name for the Honour School of Literae Humaniores ("humane letters"), which was the classic Oxford humanities course of Greek and Latin literature, history, and philosophy. He would have to pass two major examinations in this course, the Classical Moderations ("mods") in his fifth term, and the Final Schools ("schools") in another seven terms. With an honors degree, he would stand a good chance of finding some kind of academic employment; with luck, he would be elected a fellow of his college and spend the rest of his life passing along the knowledge he was now relatively busy acquiring.

In retrospect, with the image of J.R.R. Tolkien, the quintessential twentieth-century Oxford don so well established—pottering from tutorial to Senior Common Room (the lounge where fellows congregated) with a pipe fixed in his teeth and his eye fixed on an unseen horizon as he works out some esoteric textual point in *Beowulf* or ponders the Indo-European roots of the word "wasp"—it is hard to imagine Tolkien as a somewhat feckless undergraduate. The fact of the matter is, Tolkien was extraordinarily gifted as a linguist and philologist and learned this kind of material fairly easily, but he was not what in those days was called a "grind," the kind of student who spends every waking hour poring over his books in the library in the belief that accumulating a hoard of facts was the key to wisdom. Tolkien was a good student when he was interested in the topic, and he studied because he was genuinely interested in finding out more about the topic at hand. When there were other things at hand that interested him more—like Edith—he was inclined to slack off on the studying.

The first two terms that Tolkien was at Exeter College, there was no one available to serve as his tutor in classics, and so he was more or less left to his own devices. These tended more towards playing rugby and joining clubs such as the Essay Club, the Dialectical Society, and the debating society, than towards keeping his nose to the academic grindstone. He started a club of his own, devoted to reading papers, holding debates, and general discussion over indulgent dinners and after-dinner tobacco. The club was, in fact, called the Apolausticks, which means "those devoted to self-indulgence"—and their activities give an idea of Tolkien's idea of self-indulgence, then and throughout his life: hanging out with a group of like-minded men in a smoke-filled dining room and talking, talking, talking. He was not averse to joining in the general undergraduate high spirits for which Oxford was notorious, either, once hijacking a bus with a friend and driving it through town, followed by a boisterous crowd of students. This type of hijinks was called "ragging" and was generally looked on with a watchful yet indulgent eye by the university authorities. Consequences could range from a small fine to expulsion—being "sent down"—when the frolics crossed the line from youthful exuberance to dangerous or dishonorable escapades.

GOING GOTHIC

Part of Tolkien's problem in settling down to study Latin and Greek was that he was rather bored with those languages. The sensual pleasure he got from the sounds and shapes of words was no longer there for him. His imagination was increasingly drawn to northern, Germanic languages: Middle English and Anglo-Saxon, and also Gothic, the language spoken by some of the very barbarian hordes who had brought about the fall of Rome. Gothic, which only died out in the sixteenth century, is the earliest attested Germanic language, spoken by a people who had lived in the region of the Black Sea until they were forced out towards the Balkans by the Huns in the fourth century. At this time, a West Gothic bishop named Ulfilas created an alphabet for the Gothic language and used it to translate parts of the Bible.

Tolkien had first encountered Gothic when he was still at King Edward's. A school friend had, for some reason, picked up at a missionary sale a copy of the *Primer of the Gothic Language* (1892) by Joseph Wright. Finding himself in possession of a grammar of an obscure language with a minimal vocabulary and no practical usefulness, he had the bright idea of selling it to Ronald Tolkien, the school's notorious language maven. Before long, Tolkien was delivering Debating Society orations in language and in character as a Gothic envoy—impressive, but somewhat useless in terms of debate, since no one else could understand what he was saying. (On other occasions, he had debated in Greek and in Anglo-Saxon. Despite his later claim to dislike theater, Tolkien, at least as a youth, had a bent for drama.) The fascinating thing about Gothic, as far as Tolkien was concerned, was that there was enough of it to figure out how it worked, the grammar, sentence structure, and word formation, but there were huge gaps in what survived. He amused himself by inventing new Gothic words to fill in the blanks. It was his first real step towards constructing his own private language with a grammar and vocabulary not based on English or Latin. From Gothic, Tolkien moved on to inventing his own Germanic-type language from scratch, and so thorough was he, and so fascinated by the processes of comparative philology, that he invented not only a "contemporary" vocabulary for his language, he also constructed imaginary hypothetical roots for his words, much as philologists reconstruct the Indo-European roots of modern English words.[3]

While Tolkien was drifting away from the classics in his first year at Oxford, he had chosen comparative philology as an elective, which was taught by none other than Joseph Wright, the author of the Gothic grammar that had so inspired Tolkien at King Edward's. Wright was an anomaly at turn-of-the-century Oxford, which was still very much the stomping grounds of the upper class. Wright was born into a working-class family in Yorkshire in 1855, sent to work in a woolen mill at the age of six, and did not even learn to read until he was fifteen. Once he was inspired to teach himself to read, he was insatiable, attending night classes while still working at the mill and teaching his illiterate workmates to read out of a sense of duty to pass on his knowledge. The mill closed in 1876, throwing him out of work, but with his small savings he made his way, by boat and on foot, to the University of Heidelberg, where he arrived in 1876. Heidelberg is the oldest German university, founded in 1386, and was, in the late nineteenth century, one of the premier universities of Europe, with an impressive reputation in the fields of law, philosophy, and science. In the 1870s, exactly when Wright arrived at Heidelberg, German philologists who became known as *Junggrammatiker* or Neogrammarians were developing a new school of thought regarding the way sounds shift over time as a language evolves. For instance, the English inter a dead body in a "grave"; Germans put it in a "Grab." Somewhere along the line, the English sound shifted from a "b" to a "v". What the Neogrammarians proposed was that when a language underwent a sound shift like this, *all* "b's" turned into "v's", or at least, all of the sounds in a particular class, such as all the "b's" at the end of a word after a vowel, shifted to "v", and that as a result, it was possible to compare the history of sound shifts and then extrapolate them backwards to construct the hypothetical roots of words. In this case, "grave" and "Grab" derive from an Indo-European root, *ghrebh-*[2], which has produced words relating to digging, scratching, and burying. (Roots and words that are hypothetical or reconstructed are always preceded by an asterisk, to distinguish them from words that are actually found in the written record.) Joseph Wright was only able to spend eleven weeks in Heidelberg on his first visit, but he managed to get back in 1882. He studied this new school of philological thought under Professor Hermann Osthoff, receiving his doctorate in 1885. In 1891, one year before Tolkien's birth, Wright became assistant professor of comparative philology at Oxford, where he remained for the rest of his life.

Tolkien, making up his private languages in school, had been playing with the same methodologies used by comparative philologists in reconstructing roots of long-dead languages. Studying comparative philology with Wright gave him the opportunity to do it for real, and to learn from a real master. He may also have felt more at home with the down-to-earth Wright, who never forgot his factory roots in the ivory-tower atmosphere of Oxford, than he did in the more aristocratic environs of classics, which always carried a whiff of the leisured class about it. Tolkien's own background was not nearly as working-class as Wright's, but both came from the stratum of society that knew what it meant to have to struggle to get the funds for an education, rather than having it handed to them. Under Wright's tuition, Tolkien regained his sense of academic purpose.

THE ROOTS OF ELVISH

Joseph Wright encouraged Tolkien to investigate Welsh, to go beyond the pretty sounds that had caught his attention as a schoolboy and learn what the words meant. Thus, Tolkien made his first acquaintance with the bizarre and colorful world of medieval Welsh literature, where men turn into deer, boars, wolves, and back into men, where poets invoke the trees themselves to beat their branches in mourning for the death of king, where a giant wades across the Irish Sea to rescue his sister from an abusive marriage, a language whose poetry is based on the premise "take care of the sounds, and the sense will take care of itself" (as Lewis Carroll said in *Alice in Wonderland*). Welsh poetry is based on a system of alliteration and internal rhyme, and it is more important to conform to this *cynghanedd* (pronounced "kung-hahn-eth," which means, literally, "chiming together") than to create a logical or even syntactically lucid line. The piling on of sounds and words is supposed to evoke, rather than elucidate, the poet's meaning. The language's own love of its sounds resonated with Tolkien's sense of linguistic enchantment. He once tried to explain the charm of Welsh for him by saying, "Most English-speaking people ... will admit that *cellar door* is 'beautiful,' especially if dissociated from its sense (and its spelling). More beautiful than, say, *sky,* and far more beautiful than *beautiful.* Well then, in Welsh for me *cellar doors* are extraordinarily frequent."[4] As he continued to play with inventing languages, Welsh became the basis for what turned into Sindarin, his elvish language whose grammar is almost identical to that of medieval Welsh.

Tolkien also began to teach himself Finnish, which is a non-Indo-European language related to Hungarian and some of the languages of northern Siberia, as well as to Turkish and other Central Asian languages. It is another remarkably musical language, composed of long, loping words that sound like a river rushing over rocks. Tolkien had encountered the Finnish national epic, the *Kalevala,* while in school, and was eager to read it in the original. The unfamiliar grammatical system made it tough going—Finnish is what is called an agglutinating language, which means that those long, musical words are more like complete sentences in and of themselves, composed of a large number of grammatical elements "glued" together. Tolkien was never able to get completely through the *Kalevala* on his own, but he was inspired enough to use Finnish as the basis for yet another constructed language, which he eventually called Quenya.

In learning these new languages, Tolkien was spending a lot of time reading the mythologies of these cultures. There has always been a close link between comparative and historical linguistics on the one hand, and the study of mythology on the other. In part this is because mythology tends to be one of the earliest types of literature to be preserved, because it is culturally important information. Therefore, philologists who spend their days combing through ancient texts looking for ancient words have to look at those words in context to figure out what the words really mean. Mythology, however, is often a collection of very strange tales, and trying to figure out what the words mean usually leads to trying to figure out what the story itself means. (One of the nineteenth–century German philologists who first started theorizing about sound shifts, for instance, was none other than Jakob Grimm, the fairy tale collector.)

Nonetheless, Tolkien's inability to apply himself to subjects that did not enthrall him revealed itself yet again when he had to take his first set of exams, Honours Moderations, which are graded from First to Fourth Class, which might be roughly translated as "brilliant," "good," "acceptable," and "failing" grades. Tolkien managed to achieve a Second Class in his classics exams, which was good but not particularly promising for an aspiring academic. However, his exam in comparative philology was a "pure alpha" First, practically perfect in every way. The head of Exeter College suggested to Tolkien that perhaps he should consider changing from classics to English and become a philologist. With no doubt a great deal of relief, Tolkien agreed. For someone destined to become a university professor, it seemed a wise choice for Tolkien to focus on studying the subject he was best at and loved the most.

LOVERS' REUNION

While Tolkien was finding his true intellectual love at Oxford, however, he had not forgotten his true romantic love. He had promised Father Morgan that he would have no contact whatsoever with Edith until he came of age at twenty-one, and he stuck to his word, down to the letter. At 12:01 A.M. the night he turned twenty-one, January 3, 1913, the very instant he was released from his promise, he sat down and wrote to Edith, proposing marriage.

The answer he received was not, on the face of it, encouraging. Edith replied that she was engaged to George Field, the brother of her school friend Molly, whose presence in Cheltenham had helped persuade Edith to relocate there. However, Edith also said that she had become engaged to Field because she had felt this might be her only chance at marriage, not believing that Tolkien would still be in love with her after a separation of three years. She had perhaps not given the Tolkien tradition of long separation of lovers in the face of family opposition its due weight: Whether he realized it or not, Father Morgan had created a situation in which Tolkien was able to replicate almost exactly the separation his parents endured before they were finally able to marry. Whatever Father Morgan's intentions, it seems probable that one reason Tolkien was so constant in his love for Edith was that he held his parents' lives as his example; his mother had waited for his father; his father had left the country specifically to fulfill Mabel's family's requirements for a suitable husband for their daughter; he saw himself as fulfilling the same kind of service to win Edith; and he would do his best to persuade Edith to play her assigned part in this romance.

On January 8, therefore, Tolkien took the train to Cheltenham to meet with Edith, and by the end of the day, they were engaged. Edith returned the ring to George Field and weathered the storm of reproach and indignation this act produced. Tolkien returned to Oxford to take his Moderations and to write to Father Morgan announcing his reunion with his true love. Fortunately, Father Morgan realized that the time had come to throw in the towel as far as interfering with Tolkien's romantic life went and accepted the engagement. He was no longer legally responsible for Tolkien as a guardian, but he still regarded himself as morally responsible for the young man and also was providing financial support to make up the difference between Tolkien's exhibition money and his actual expenses. His acceptance of the engagement was important.

While Edith was willing to endure the social consequences of giving up her fiancé, the question of giving up her religion was somewhat more contentious. Tolkien was adamant that she must convert to Catholicism. For him, there was no question about this. His own faith was one of the defining aspects of his identity, and his belief that his mother had been essentially martyred for their religion made any thought of his leaving the Catholic church utterly out of the question. However, although the ideal in Edwardian England was for families to be unified in their religious adherence, it was not unusual when one member belonged to a Nonconformist religion for the family to be divided in its faith. Tolkien's own grandfather John Suffield had been a Unitarian in a family of Methodists. There was no reason why the Tolkiens could not have come to an agreement to go their separate ways, religiously speaking, making some kind of compact on the religion in which to raise their children.

Edith was an Anglican largely out of convenience rather than faith. The Anglican church was, after all, the default religion of the English people. She did not care for confession, and she did not appear to need spiritual comfort from the church, whether Anglican or Catholic. Her religion was important to her as a focus of her social life, as the parish church often was in English society, but it was also important to her as an outlet for her musical talents, allowing her a chance to play the organ for services. Her participation in parish activities gave her social status. It also pleased the Jessops, the couple with whom she was living. To convert to Catholicism would make her an outcast, just as it had done to Mabel Tolkien. Tolkien's asking Edith to convert seems to have been, at least in part, motivated by a desire to make his life parallel that of his parents, to make his future wife recapitulate his mother's life. In many ways, Edith shared Mabel's independent spirit and lively personality. Mabel, however, had converted to prove her love for God; Edith was being asked to convert as a kind of test of her love for Tolkien. She did it, but not happily.

As Edith feared, the announcement to the Jessops of her impending conversion was not well received. Mr. Jessop, a man she had heretofore called "Uncle," demanded that she leave his house as soon as she could find new accommodation. Perhaps as a statement of her independence, Edith decided to move not to Oxford, where she would be near Tolkien, but to Warwick, a town near Birmingham. There, in the spring of 1913, she set up house with her cousin Jennie Grove, the woman who had lived with Edith and her mother during Edith's childhood. The only problem was that the Catholic priest in Warwick turned out to be rather uninterested in preparing Edith for her conversion, a situation unlikely to endear the process to her. She began to feel hardly used. She seemed to be making all the sacrifices, while Tolkien lived the life of the ivory tower. Furthermore, although her new fiancé sincerely loved her and while his prospects certainly were much improved since their teenage years at Mrs. Faulkener's, the three years of their separation had seen them grow in different directions. Tolkien had always kept his romantic life hidden from his male companions, which had made it very easy, during the years of enforced noncommunication, simply to act as though that side of his life did not exist. Similarly, the bond between Tolkien and Edith had always been emotional rather than intellectual, and although she might accept the fact that Tolkien's intellectual talents were likely to provide him with a means to make a living as a teacher or professor, even to the end of their lives she never participated in that side of his personality. From Tolkien's point of view, the companion with whom he had shared all his sorrows in their adolescence had become an independent young lady with domestic interests. The minutiae of housekeeping and of local society bored him out of his wits.

A MIDLANDS MAN

While Edith was settling into Warwick, Tolkien was settling into the school of English Language and Literature. His new tutor, Kenneth Sisam, specialized in Anglo-Saxon and Middle English, two fields close to Tolkien's heart. At about the time that Tolkien began studying with him, Sisam was working on an edition of the lay of Havelok the Dane, an orphan cast adrift by his guardians to prevent him from taking his rightful throne. (Naturally, he is found by a kind-hearted fisherman, eventually reclaims his throne, and rewards his foster father—happy endings all around.) Although Tolkien had already read many of the texts that Sisam assigned him, his new tutor focused his attention on linguistic problems in the evolution of Anglo-Saxon dialects into Middle English. It was about this time that Tolkien started to embrace the Midlands dialect of Middle English as particularly his own, not only as a topic of academic study, but as his ancestral tongue, the language spoken by the ancient Suffields.

Among the texts Tolkien now read was the poem *Crist* by a seventh-century Anglo-Saxon poet named Cynewulf, the earliest named poet in English literature. The earliest surviving manuscript of *Crist* appears in the eleventh-century Exeter Book, severely damaged and missing the first part of the poem. However, the second part of this three-part poem contains the poet's "signature," his name written in Germanic runic letters rather than the Roman alphabet of the text. Although Cynewulf's poetry was almost entirely religious, in the early twentieth century it was believed that he might also be the author of the collection of ninety-some Anglo-Saxon riddles also found in the Exeter Book.[5] In the poem *Crist*, Tolkien also came across the lines "*éala! éarendel engla beorhtast ofer middangeard monnum sended*" ("Hail! [Earendel], brightest of angels thou, sent unto men upon this middle-earth").[6] Years later, in a draft letter replying to a query about the sources of his names in his fiction, Tolkien recalled that when he stumbled across the word *éarendel* in his earliest days of studying Anglo-Saxon, it immediately impressed him with its beauty. The context of the word suggests that it refers to a star or constellation and so, within a year, he was writing a poem in which "Eärendil" became the name of a hero who, in standard mythological apotheosis, became an eternal mariner in the sky, bringing hope to those who saw him.[7] In a footnote within his draft letter, Tolkien notes that the word *éorendel* is applied to John the Baptist in the *Blickling Homilies* (a late-tenth-century collection of sermons and religious narratives), and seems to refer to the Baptist as a herald of Christ. Cynewulf's poem *Andreas*, a story of St. Andrew's missionary activities, shows a deep familiarity with seafaring, another Cynewulfian characteristic that Tolkien adopted in his image of Eärendil.

Tolkien was rapidly expanding his knowledge of European languages: by this time, he was able to read English in all its historic manifestations, French, Spanish, German, Latin, Greek, Gothic, Welsh, Finnish, and Old Norse. However, in the summer of 1913 he took a job as a tutor and escort to two Mexican boys who were to travel through France with another boy and two of their aunts, all of them Spanish-speaking, with little or no English. Tolkien was somewhat dismayed to discover that not only was his meager Spanish inadequate for communicating with his charges—he had mostly learned it through exposure to Father Morgan's own Spanish heritage—but his French was completely useless for practical travel needs. This is a common situation when one learns a language "academically," where the emphasis is on being able to read literary criticism (a genre that usually has its own arcane vocabulary completely disconnected from the real world) and original literary texts, as opposed to learning a language "conversationally," where the emphasis is on speaking and, more importantly, being able to recognize words by their sounds in the air rather than their appearance on the page. Comprehending a spoken language requires a certain amount of speed and almost unconscious recognition of words; people speak quickly (and a foreign language often sounds as though it is being spoken at an amazingly fast pace to someone whose comprehension is limited) and there is no time to look one word up in the dictionary before the next one is spoken. Tolkien's linguistic embarrassment contributed to his general dislike for all things French—he loved the city of Paris but increasingly despised the people. Later in life, Tolkien stated that "I detest French cooking," contrasting it with "good plain food (unrefrigerated)."[8] It seems likely that his culinary antipathy dates to this trip.

It was a great contrast to Tolkien's previous Continental experience, a trip to the Swiss Alps he and his brother Hilary, along with their Aunt Jane and another family, had taken during the summer before he entered Oxford, where they camped out and hiked. That trip had seen a near-disaster when the group was overtaken by an avalanche of rocks loosened by melting snowpack that nearly knocked Tolkien off of the narrow mountain path. However, Tolkien regarded the event as a piece of adventure in the context of a happy holiday. The French trip was not so pleasantly concluded.

The group took a side trip to Brittany, an area Tolkien was eager to see since its native language, Breton, is closely related to Welsh. However, they spent all their time in Dinard, a completely charmless seaside resort populated by nothing but tourists like themselves. But genuine calamity struck one day when, as Tolkien, one of his charges, and one of the aunts were walking along the street, the aunt was run down by a car that drove up onto the sidewalk. The holiday ended with Tolkien making arrangements to ship her body back to Mexico and seeing the rest of the family off.

THE CALM BEFORE THE STORM

Returning to the safety of Oxford, Tolkien was happy to be joined at the university by his T.C.B.S. companion G. B. Smith, who was resident at Corpus Christi College, Oxford, but was also reading English. R. Q. Gilson and Christopher Wiseman, for their parts, were settled at Cambridge University, but the four friends did not let the traditional rivalry between England's grandest universities keep them from maintaining contact and meeting when they could manage it. Meanwhile, Edith was still preparing for her entrance into the Catholic Church in Warwick. The time was approaching for Tolkien to bring together the two halves of his life, the academic and the romantic. His announcement of his engagement to his fellow T.C.B.S.-ites was received with congratulations, but seemingly with little comprehension. Edith, for her part, was becoming irritated at receiving letters from her fiancé relating his life of dinner parties and movie-going, college clubs and debating, and tennis and punting. Nonetheless, on January 8, 1914, the first anniversary of their reunion, Edith was received into the Catholic Church, and soon afterward the couple's engagement was made official.

The rest of the academic year passed happily for Tolkien. He was not so caught up in the university social whirl—nor, for once, so distracted by the complexities of his romantic life—as to neglect his studies, and the wisdom of his decision to switch from Greats to English was confirmed when he won the Skeat Prize for English. He used the prize money to buy books of medieval Welsh and also some of the "medieval romances" based on Germanic mythology written by William Morris. Morris—who had also been an undergraduate at Exeter College—was a late-Victorian polymath who turned his hand equally to socialist politics, interior decor, publishing, and novel writing. He is today perhaps best known as one of the guiding lights of the artistic movement known as Arts and Crafts, whose signature style was a return to the handmade aesthetic of preindustrial manufacture (he was the designer of the Morris chair, today considered the archetypal piece of "Mission"-style furniture). Morris's literary efforts were equally medievalist, recreating the life of Dark Age Europe in a hybrid style of prose and poetry that recalled the structure of the early epics; they were, in essence, modern novels written *as* the medieval tales that Tolkien was studying. For a man who claimed rarely to read a novel, Morris's stories opened up a new world of narrative possibilities, a way to integrate the premodern mentality into a modern genre.

During the Long Vacation of 1914, Tolkien visited Cornwall with one of the priests from the Birmingham Oratory. They spent their time walking through the countryside around the Lizard Peninsula, and Tolkien was especially taken with the well-known beauty of the rough Cornish coast, rocky and windswept, everlastingly pounded by the Atlantic surf. The Lizard is the location of Land's End, the most westerly point of mainland Britain; a sailor setting due west from this port would not hit land until he reached North America. Cornwall is also one of the Celtic areas of Britain, although Cornish, another language closely related to Welsh, had almost ceased to be spoken since the eighteenth century. Cornwall is rich in folklore of giants, mermaids, and numerous "little peoples" such as piskies, spriggans, and knockers. And off to the west of Land's End is said to lie the lost city of Lyonesse, a British Atlantis overwhelmed by the sea during the time of King Arthur; the Scilly Islands are said to be the sole remains of this rich and beautiful land, the tips of former mountains that alone emerge from the waves. The hero Tristan, whose doomed love affair with Iseult was one of the most famous stories of Arthurian romance, was a prince of Lyonesse left exiled by his land's inundation. Folklore held that the bells of Lyonesse's many churches can still be heard ringing beneath stormy seas. The landscape and legends of Cornwall long remained in Tolkien's heart as his ideal. However, what was universally agreed to have been one of the most perfect summers in European memory was about to be overwhelmed, like Lyonesse, in a stormy sea of world events. On June 28, 1914, the heir apparent of the Austro-Hungarian Empire, Archduke Franz Ferdinand, was assassinated by a Serbian nationalist while on a visit to Sarajevo; international events spiraled out of control as Austria-Hungary declared war on Serbia on July 28; Russia mobilized in support of its ally, causing Germany to declare war on Russia August 1 and on France August 3; the German invasion of Belgium, en route to France, on August 4 brought Great Britain into the fray; and by the time Michaelmas Term began in the autumn of 1914, World War I was barreling down like a juggernaut on an entire generation.

NOTES

1. Allen, Carleton Kemp, "College Life," in *Handbook to the University of Oxford* (Oxford: Clarendon Press, 1932), 104.

2. C.S. Lewis, *The Letters of C. S. Lewis*, edited, with a memoir, by W.H. Lewis; revised and enlarged edition edited by Walter Hooper (London: Collins, 1988), 285.

3. *The American Heritage Dictionary of Indo-European Roots* by Calvert Watkins (Boston: Houghton Mifflin, 1985), which also appears as an appendix at the end of the *American Heritage Dictionary*, shows the hypothesized Indo-European roots of many modern English words, illustrating how a root evolves and changes its meaning over time. Watkins's introduction is a clear exposition of how comparative philology works.

4. Carpenter, *Biography*, 64.

5. See Craig Williamson, *A Feast of Creatures: Anglo-Saxon Riddle-Songs* (Philadelphia: University of Pennsylvania Press, 1982).

6. Israel Gollancz, ed. and trans., *Cynewulf's Christ: An Eighth Century English Epic*. London: D. Nutt, 1892.

7. Carpenter, *Letters*, 385.

8. Carpenter, *Letters*, 288–89.

Chapter 4

THE END OF THE THIRD AGE (1914–1918)

The first predictions were that the war would be over by Christmas. Public feeling in Britain was strongly in favor of intervening in what might have otherwise been dismissed as an affair of purely Continental interest, largely because of Germany's gratuitous violation of Belgium's neutrality and the truly valiant decision of the Belgians to stand up for their sovereignty and their principles by refusing to allow Germany simply to sweep through on their way to invading France. Germany, for its part, had convinced itself not only of its moral right to invade, but also that all other European countries were conspiring to thwart Germany from taking its true place on the world stage.[1] The impulses that led Britons to enlist sprang from truly Victorian values of fair play, moral rectitude, and a belief in the overall reliability of the people in authority; what David Lloyd George, the Welsh politician who was to become prime minister from 1916 to 1922, in a speech given on September 19, 1914, called "the great peaks ... of Honour, Duty, Patriotism, and, clad in glittering white, the great pinnacle of Sacrifice pointing like a rugged finger to Heaven."[2] The war did not turn out to be the War to End All Wars, as those who became irrevocably involved in fighting it tried to claim, but it did become the war to end this kind of faith, a war to make Lloyd George's rhetoric impossible to hear with a straight face.

Perhaps the most significant clue to the cultural impact of the Great War was that it could be called a "world war." The last wars to be fought on this scale were the wars of Napoleon, almost exactly a century before; in fact, much of the politics that caused this war, including the antagonisms among Germany, France, and Russia, were festering resentments left over from the redistribution of European power that resulted from the Napoleonic wars. Nonetheless, although the repercussions of those nineteenth-century wars were felt throughout Europe and into the Middle East and North America, the mentality that would allow them to be called "world wars" was not yet in existence. There was a sense that World War I, the first (and it was hoped, the last) major war of the twentieth century, was going to be a kind of millennial war, clearing away the cultural deadwood and making the way for a progressive, modern future, a new and hopeful world.

It is interesting that, for all his romantic adventurousness and his immersion in the heroic ethos of medieval warrior sagas, Tolkien was not particularly eager to enlist. Perhaps he was already aware of the fact that warrior sagas rarely have happy endings; the best end for a warrior is to die in battle and to live forever only in legend. Tolkien finally had very tangible things to live for: He was engaged to the woman he had suffered for in silence for three years, he was making a reputation for himself at university, and he had every prospect of being able to make a reasonable living for himself and his potential family in a field that he loved. Yet Oxford was practically deserted, bereft of almost every man who was physically fit for service. However, Tolkien soon discovered a program whereby he could join the Officer Training Corps and still stay on at university until he had finished his degree. He found "digs," rented rooms outside the college, which he shared with a classmate who was not eligible for the army due to his bad health, and settled in to study and drill. Perhaps the one advantage of his situation was that, with all his former companions off to war, he had no distractions to keep him from study.

POETS PREPARE FOR WAR

Tolkien was also amusing himself with trying to write a Morris-esque romance based on the Finnish epic the *Kalevala* (although it ultimately remained unfinished). Over the Christmas holidays of 1914, the core members of the T.C.B.S.—Tolkien, Wiseman, Gilson, and Smith—had gathered at the Wisemans' house in Wandsworth. No doubt the pall of their impending military service hung over the reunion, but their conversation mainly centered on their shared artistic ambitions. Although there are no specific accounts of what they discussed that weekend, Tolkien came away with a conviction not only that his role in life was to be a poet, but that the group as a whole had committed themselves to a kind of artistic brotherhood with common goals. Tolkien compared this late incarnation of the T.C.B.S. to the Pre-Raphaelite Brotherhood, the group of poets and painters including William Morris, Dante Gabriel Rossetti and his sister Christina, Sir Edward Burne-Jones, William Holman Hunt, and John Everett Millais. That group had chosen their name to reflect their interest in the arts of Europe prior to the lifetime of the Italian Renaissance painter Raphael (1483–1520), considered a master of Neoplatonic realism, as opposed to the formalism of medieval and early Renaissance painting. The Pre-Raphaelites, then, turned their backs on the movement towards realism, Reformation, and rationality that had characterized the modern world, and Tolkien's comparison of the T.C.B.S. to them suggests that the artistic goals of the T.C.B.S. were similarly medievalist. (Or at least, his goals were—the Pre-Raphaelite comparison was disparaged by the others.) What was important was that this common artistic vision gave Tolkien an outlet for "all kind of pent-up things" ;[3] perhaps he was finally able to voice to his friends the emotions underlying his romance with Edith.

In any case, on his return to Oxford, Tolkien began producing poetry at a rather rapid clip, sending the drafts off to his companions for critique. Most often, their advice was that he needed to restrain himself, to avoid excessive emotionalism and overblown diction. Smith suggested that Tolkien might profit from reading some of the poetry of Rupert Brooke, the charismatic soldier-poet whose cycle of sonnets published in December 1914 promised that should he die in battle (which he did, five months later), "there's some corner of a foreign field / That's forever England." Tolkien, however, was not impressed with modern English poetry; in fact, he was starting to write his poetry in his own invented languages. Once again, his attraction was to the sound of the words almost more than the sense of the poem. He began to formulate a mythological background for his languages—after all, he had learned other languages through reading their mythologies—that focused on a poem inspired by Cynewulf's reference to Éarendel. In Tolkien's vision, the mariner sailed through the sky until he came to a land of elves; his Welsh- and Finnish-based languages became the languages of the elves.

By the middle of June 1915, Tolkien had sat for and passed his Schools exams and received a First Class Honours degree. His career as an academic was assured, if only he could survive the war. This was beginning to seem increasingly unlikely. Once his exams were over, the deferral of Tolkien's commission as a second lieutenant in the Lancashire Fusiliers (the same regiment as his friend Smith, although they were assigned to different battalions) came to an end, and the simple drilling in the vicinity of Oxford that he had been carrying out was replaced by serious military training at a series of camps around the country. He went halves with another officer on the purchase of a motorcycle so that he could travel from wherever he was currently posted to visit Edith. He decided to learn signaling, since it was an opportunity to at least learn more "languages"—Morse code, flag and disc signaling, heliograph and lamp messaging, signal rockets, the operation of field telephones, and the use of carrier pigeons—otherwise, he found training unbearably dull.

THE DEATH OF A GENERATION

It was already becoming clear, despite the heavy censorship of letters from the front and of news reports, that this was going to be not only a long but a bloody war. By the end of 1914, nearly the entire British Expeditionary Force of 160,000 men sent to France had been killed.[4] By the end of the war, of the British Empire's 8.9 million soldiers, 3.2 million had been killed or wounded—nearly 36 percent of the entire mobilized force.[5] In many ways, the ones who died were the lucky ones. Military technology had advanced to a stage where it was possible to blow people to ever tinier pieces, but medical technology had not yet advanced to be able to sew them back together again in any functioning way. Those who lost body parts to shrapnel lived the rest of their lives with arms, legs, ears, noses, eyes, or fingers missing. Gas warfare destroyed men's lungs and caused permanent brain damage. Machine guns mowed down lines of soldiers, who advanced across the muddy fields of northern France in slow, deliberate ranks, with such ruthless efficiency that the gunners could hardly believe their eyes—not only that the enemy set themselves up for such carnage, but that having done it once, having seen the results, they persisted in doing it again and again. For the first time, airplanes were used to drop bombs from above, rather than firing shells from afar through cannon.

After Christmas of 1914, the war settled down into an unbearable stalemate, with opposing forces spending most of their time hunkered down in trenches. The world closed in to a deep, narrow alley, and sunlight only penetrated these manmade gullies for the few minutes a day that the sun was directly overhead. Otherwise, the place was damp and muddy and crawling with vermin—especially fleas, which seemed to reproduce at a demonic rate and were a primary vector for spreading "trench fever," and rats that grew to the size of cats and devoured not only any food they could gnaw their way into, but also the unburied corpses that littered the landscape. In the No-Man's Land that lay between opposing trenches, the field where battle actually took place, enemy snipers made it impossible to retrieve the bodies of the dead, who were left to decompose in the ever-present rain. As the war progressed, any disturbance of the soil—such as a battalion of soldiers marching across the field—churned up bodies and body parts that rose from the earth like the undead.

The experience contrasted unbearably with the noble impulses that had led most men to enlist in the army, and as soldiers became sickeningly numbed to the grind—three or four days in the frontline trenches, another three or four in the support trenches further back, and then three or four days in reserve—they developed an increasing resentment of the commanders, who quite evidently had no idea what those at the front were experiencing. That lack of first-hand experience of the horrors the common soldiers were enduring was blamed unequivocally on the cowardice of those who had managed to wangle themselves safe desk jobs.[6] Even worse was the incomprehension of those left at home, who were fed an unending stream of official propaganda extolling the noble endeavors of the military and who received only heavily censored letters from the front. Not that there was much to be said in those letters, anyway; soldiers found themselves trapped in a situation that was literally indescribable, and so by and large they did not even try. Even the most well-meaning responses from civilians struck the soldiers at the front as simply fatuous.

TOLKIEN IN FRANCE

This was the world Tolkien was about to enter, straight from the ivory towers of Oxford. He and Edith decided that it would be best for them to marry before he left for the front. Their main reason was that they had waited long enough to marry and they should have that happiness, at least, before Tolkien went off to a war from which he very likely would not return. However, there was also the question of setting his affairs in order so that what little money he had would go to Edith in the event of his death. Tolkien arranged to have the inheritance that Father Morgan held in trust for him transferred to his own name, but he could not bring himself to tell his former guardian that he was finally getting married to the woman that Father Morgan had so opposed. Tolkien broke the news by letter a mere two weeks before the wedding and was relieved to receive Father Morgan's blessing on the union. They were married on March 22, 1916, in the Warwick church that Edith attended, and spent a week-long honeymoon in Clevedon, Somerset. Edith gave up her house in Warwick, and she and Jennie Grove prepared themselves for a peripatetic life as camp followers, trailing after Tolkien wherever he happened to be posted. Edith and Jennie had found themselves furnished rooms in Great Haywood, in Staffordshire, and had just settled in when Tolkien received his embarkation orders for France. On June 4, 1916, a bare two-and-a-half months after his wedding, he was off to war.

He managed to lose his entire kit en route to France—a rather expensive, for him, assemblage of camping-type furniture that would make life in the trenches merely unbearable rather than simply insupportable—and had to replace it all. When he finally arrived in Étaples, his base camp, he followed the standard procedure of sitting around for days with nothing to do. He was transferred to the Eleventh Battalion, where he found himself markedly out of character with the other officers, who were divided between young recruits who, like himself, were completely inexperienced in war, and older veterans who were pleased to take any opportunity to expose the youngsters' military naivete. On the whole, Tolkien found that it was the N.C.O.s (non-commissioned officers) and privates who had their heads screwed on straight, and the protocol of the British military prevented him from socializing with them. These were men of working-class and lower-middle-class background, probably closer to what Tolkien himself would have been if he had not made it to university by means of his brains, and perhaps in many ways more like his brother Hilary, who had already left farming to enlist as a bugler. After three weeks, the battalion left Étaples for the Somme and the "Big Push" that was supposed to end the war in one fell swoop.

The Battle of the Somme lasted from July 1 to November 13, 1916. On the first day, twenty thousand British troops were killed and forty thousand wounded, still the largest loss in a single day that the British army has ever suffered; there were more than half a million casualties before the battle was over. At the end of three-and-one-half months, the Allied forces had advanced barely five miles. "The battles of Verdun, the Somme, and Ypres embody the logic, the meaning, the essence of the Great War," Modris Eksteins comments. "And the standard imagery that we have of the Great War—the deafening, enervating artillery barrages, the attacks in which long lines of men move forward as in slow motion over a moonscape of craters and mud, only to confront machine guns, uncut barbed wire, and grenades—come from these battles .... This middle part of the war reversed all traditional notions of warfare."[7] At the end of the twentieth century, farm fields that had been battlefields still could not be plowed without turning up human bones.

The Germans defended their posts with tangles of barbed wire. It had been assumed that the week of artillery bombardment that the French and English engaged in before sending in foot soldiers would have caused heavy casualties among the Germans and blasted the wire to shreds. Unfortunately—and as another example of the lack of real-world knowledge on the part of the men in charge—neither occurred. The artillery in fact merely tossed the wire up into the air, allowing it to settle down in more of a tangle than before, creating an impenetrable boundary that caught what few Allied soldiers that had not already been mowed down. Some were killed by friendly fire, as Allied shells fell short of their targets onto their own advancing army.

THE WASTELAND

On June 28, Tolkien's battalion took the train from Étaples to Amiens and then marched on foot to the front. Along the way, it began to rain—incessant rain was one of the curses of this war's battlefields—and the road turned to mud. After ten miles, they reached the small village of Rubempré, where they spent the night, the men camped in sheds and barns, the officers on camp beds set up in what farmhouses had not already been blasted by shelling. The Allies were already bombarding the German lines, "softening them up" for the planned infantry offensive. The Eleventh Lancashire Fusiliers were not to be in the first line of troops to go "over the top" (describing the action of scrambling out of the underground trenches onto the battlefield) on the first day of battle; they were held in reserve to sweep in after the Germans, fragmented and demoralized by the two weeks of shelling, crumbled before the first offensive. Tolkien's battalion was supposed to have a clear field in front of them to push through the former German front line and thrust deeply into enemy territory, breaking the stalemate that had kept the two armies sitting and staring each other down for a year.

Tolkien and his companions sat out July 1, the first day of battle, at a village called Bouzincourt, and they could see that things were not going according to plan. Men were returning from the front not just wounded but mutilated; reserves were being formed into grave-digging details. The Germans were not softened by the shelling, the barbed wire that defended their positions had not been cut, and as the Allied troops had dutifully followed their orders to march slowly in line across No-Man's Land, each man weighed down by a sixty-five-pound backpack of equipment on his back, the Germans simply mowed them down with machine-gun fire. One of the twenty thousand Allied troops killed that day was Tolkien's friend Rob (R. Q.) Gilson.

Tolkien, meanwhile, was still sitting at Bouzincourt with little to do but wonder about the fate of his friends—he knew that Gilson and Smith had gone into battle already, but had no news of their fate—and wait for his own "B" company to be sent in. Smith eventually turned up, uninjured, on July 6, and the two had a chance to catch up on news and also to distract themselves from the war around them with their ongoing literary discussions and plans.

Finally, on July 14, Tolkien's company was sent to the front. It was his first experience of an actual trench, cramped, muddy, and disorganized. Even worse, not all of the previous tenants left when the switch-over between companies took place: The dead and parts of the dead stayed behind in the corners where they died, quietly decaying in the mud as the war plodded on around them. Out in No-Man's Land, the grass had been stomped into a giant mud puddle, the trees had been stripped of their leaves, and at high summer the place looked like the bleakest part of autumn. The general aura of unseasonal decay was only enhanced by even more decomposing bodies, lying on the mud, sinking into the mud, emerging from the mud. Many of the bodies could not be buried until the battle was "over" in November.

The next day, the "B" company was sent into battle, attached to the Seventh Infantry Brigade to attempt to take the village of Ovillers from the Germans. They were not successful. It was the same story of barbed wire not cut, slow marches cut down by machine-gun fire, and many casualties. Tolkien fought for forty-eight hours without rest and somehow managed to escape with little more than cuts; he was allowed a few hours' sleep in a dugout, and then it was back to battle for another twelve hours. Finally, what remained of "B" company returned to Bouzincourt. There Tolkien found a letter from Smith telling him of Rob Gilson's death. It was news that left him feeling that he was not "a member of a complete body now."[8]

From that point, Tolkien was part of the routine of trench warfare, cycling through the phases of reserve, support trenches, and front line, mud and boredom punctuated by mud and terror. Most of Tolkien's battalion was killed, sooner or later, as the Battle of the Somme wore on, but somehow he managed to get through it all without any physical damage. He was getting accustomed to the smell of blood and decay, and he killed so that he would not be killed. It was a far cry from reading about Beowulf's battles with man-eating monsters in the comfort of his Oxford digs. He had become part of the man-eating machine.

THE HOUSES OF HEALING

Summer turned to autumn, and the misery of wet and mud was increased by the addition of bitter cold. In the end, it was not guns that got Tolkien, but disease. On October 27, he came down with something the soldiers called trench fever, and the doctors called pyrexia; in the years after the war, it was discovered that trench fever was a disease related to rickets. The symptoms of the disease, which was transmitted by the body lice that infested 97 percent of the troops, were very high fever accompanied by severe headache, pains in the muscles of the torso and legs (especially in the lumbar region of the lower back and in the neck), a characteristic pain in the shins, and often severe shivering attacks and a transient pink rash. As a general rule, the fever only lasted five or six days, followed by a remission of five or six days, but then the fever would be back; a soldier could experience up to twelve bouts of the fever-remission cycle, lasting over four months. Although trench fever was never fatal of itself, it left sufferers debilitated and clinically depressed. Aside from the trenches of both world wars, trench fever is usually found in refugee camps, homeless populations, and the scenes of natural disasters.

Tolkien was taken to a hospital at Le Touquet, but when his symptoms had not eased after a week, he was put on a transport ship and sent to a military hospital in Birmingham. Somehow, he had managed to be sent home. Edith joined him, and by the third week of December he had recovered sufficiently for her to take him back to Great Haywood, where she was still living with Jennie Grove, to spend Christmas. Once again, he returned to a place of safety to be greeted by grim news: G. B. Smith had died of shell injuries in France on December 3. His injuries had not been immediately fatal—he was wounded by shrapnel in his arm and leg—but gangrene had set in too quickly for the doctors to operate on him. The last time he and Tolkien had seen each other was in late August, when their battalions had brought them together near Bouzincourt. In one of his letters to Tolkien while they were both still in the trenches, Smith had charged him to "say the things I have tried to say long after I am not there to say them."[9] Tolkien was increasingly coming to feel that he had not only a calling but a duty to dead friends to express himself as a writer—much as he had a duty to his mother to remain a Catholic.

He therefore took advantage of his convalescence to begin writing what he hoped would be a *Kalevala* for England. (In this act alone he showed that, no matter what his talents as a teacher and scholar, he had the soul of a writer, who always regards time off the day job as a chance to finally get some real work done.) There has been some controversy about the status of the *Kalevala* as an authentic ancient epic. Elias Lönnrot, the epic's compiler, had begun by collecting individual folk songs throughout Finland. The idea of stringing them together to create a coherent episodic narrative, comparable to Homer's *Iliad* and *Odyssey*, composed of the "best" performances of each episode in his collection, was Lönnrot's own. The *Kalevala* never existed as a unified whole in the folk tradition; its "wholeness" was only achieved on Lönnrot's publication of his constructed text in 1849. Tolkien's plan for his own epic, typically, followed the pattern of his invented languages: Where Lönnrot had taken fragments and woven them together, Tolkien began by (re)constructing his own "ancient" fragments of the history of Middle-earth, which he called The Silmarillion.

By January, Tolkien was recovering and Edith was pregnant. At the end of February, however, he had a relapse that lasted three weeks. When he was well enough to travel again, he was posted to a camp in Yorkshire, and Edith and Jennie followed. Once again, Tolkien relapsed, this time so badly that he was sent to recuperate at a sanatorium at the famous spa of Harrogate. After another few weeks, he was well enough to be sent back to the camp. However, the pattern of recovery and relapse continued throughout the spring and summer, preventing him from being sent back to France but also preventing him from doing much of anything else. Edith, meanwhile, was getting bigger and bigger, living in uncomfortable rooms in the dreary seaside town of Hornsea, which had not been renowned for cheerfulness even during peacetime. With wartime restrictions on food and heat—even in summer, the Yorkshire coast is cold and wet—it was hardly any perkier. In August, Tolkien's latest relapse landed him at the Brooklands Officers' Hospital in Hull, where his fellow inmates included a friend from the Lancashire Fusiliers, and there was a convent nearby, which meant that his Catholic needs were also tended to. Edith was not so lucky—the Catholic church in Hornsea was lodged in a movie theater—and she seriously considered just going with Jennie to the Anglican church instead. In the end, she decided in September to go south instead and spend the end of her pregnancy back in Cheltenham, where she had been relatively happy when she was boarding with the Jessops. On November 16, 1917, Edith gave birth in a Cheltenham nursing home to her first child, whom she and Tolkien named John Francis Reuel Tolkien. After all of the misunderstandings between Tolkien and his former guardian—the "Francis" was for him—Father Morgan performed the baptism. Afterwards, the entire Tolkien family once again removed to Yorkshire, where Tolkien, now a full lieutenant, was posted to a camp near Roos. It was beginning to look as though he would be spending the rest of the war on British soil. His health was too precarious to send him back to the trenches.

BEREN AND LÚTHIEN

It was while they lived at Roos that the couple went on a picnic that inspired one of the central myths of Tolkien's developing Silmarillion. Years later, after Edith's death, Tolkien recalled in a letter to his son Christopher that the story of the romance between the human man Beren and the elf-maiden Lúthien "was first conceived in a small woodland glade filled with hemlocks at Roos .... In those days [Edith's] hair was raven, her skin clear, her eyes brighter than you have seen them, and she could sing—and *dance*."[10] The image of the unearthly singing of the elves, the primal innocence of the wooded setting, and the romance between two members of alien races ran throughout Tolkien's writing from then on. (It is interesting that, for all the complaints by later critics that Tolkien's female characters were relatively passive and idealized, the story of Beren and Lúthien, which he very explicitly claimed to be a mythologizing of his own relationship with Edith, features an extremely active female lead who takes matters into her own hands to assist her lover in accomplishing the quest he must fulfill to win her.)

Tolkien was posted back south to Staffordshire in the spring of 1918, at just about the same time that all the surviving members of his original battalion were either killed or taken prisoner when, on May 27, the Germans attacked Chemin des Dames, where Allied troops had, ironically, been sent to recuperate from battles in Flanders. This was yet another mismanaged battle; escaped prisoners of war had been warning the Allied forces for several days that the Germans were building up for an attack, but those who could have ordered preparations against the attack ignored the intelligence. It was hardly an opportune moment to return to the front. Yet, almost as soon as the Tolkiens had arrived at Penkridge, Tolkien was posted back to Hull. This time, Edith refused to follow him back north, and as soon as he arrived in Yorkshire, Tolkien once again suffered a relapse and was back in the hospital, where, Edith commented somewhat bitterly, he had now accumulated enough time in bed to last him the rest of his life. Tolkien was out of the hospital in October, and before he could be shunted around any more, the war, miraculously, ended. Armistice was signed on November 11, 1918, and somehow Ronald Tolkien had survived a war that had claimed the lives of nearly one third of the men who had been with him at Oxford, before that golden age of the world had come to its muddy end.

NOTES

1. Barbara Tuchman's *The Proud Tower: A Portrait of the World Before the War, 1890–1914* (New York: Macmillan, 1962), is still one of the best and most readable histories of the events leading up to World War I and the society the war destroyed. Peter Fussell's *The Great War and Modern Memory* (New York: Oxford University Press, 1975) and Modris Eksteins's *Rites of Spring: The Great War and the Birth of the Modern Age* (Boston: Houghton Mifflin, 1989) are good explorations of the cultural impact of the war.

2. Quoted in Eksteins, 132–33.

3. Carpenter, *Biography*, 81.

4. Eksteins, 100.

5. *Encyclopædia Britannica*, s.v. "World War I," http://search.eb.com/eb/article?eu=118861, accessed December 22, 2002.

6. Fussell, 82–90.

7. Eksteins, 145.

8. Carpenter, *Biography*, 92.

9. Carpenter, *Biography*, 94.

10. Carpenter, *Letters*, 420.

Chapter 5

THE YOUNG ACADEMIC
(1918–1925)

With the war over, Tolkien now had to resume the life that he had left behind in 1915. When war broke out, no one was thinking very much of what would happen afterwards: At first it was assumed that the war would be over quickly and everything would be back to normal before anyone knew it, and then, when the war's devastation on an entire generation of young men started to become clear, it was impossible to imagine what kind of world would arise from its ashes. Places that were natural focal points for young men—universities such as Oxford and Cambridge—were particularly affected. In 1914, the undergraduate enrollment at Oxford was 1,400 students; in 1916, it had dropped to 550; in 1917, 460, and in 1918, it was only 369.[1] Although the overall death rate for the British forces was around 10 percent of the total mobilized armed forces, the rate among Oxford students was closer to 30 percent.

Although peace was supposed to herald a new era free from all the hardships that had marked the war years, reality was not quite so idyllic. The winter of 1918–1919 saw an epidemic of a particularly virulent influenza that killed twice as many people as had been killed in the war. Worldwide, 27,000,000 people died of the flu; in Britain alone, the death toll was around 200,000.[2] Furthermore, despite the decimation of the adult male working population, jobs were hard to come by for many veterans, often because of the physical and psychological aftereffects of their war service. Many men were seriously disabled, some with missing limbs, others with shocking facial disfigurations, while still others suffered the effects of what was then called shell shock, a psychological state now called post-traumatic stress disorder.

WRITING THE OED

Tolkien was lucky, in that his skills were so specialized that, while he was suited for very few jobs, there was little competition for the few that did exist. On paying a call on his old Icelandic tutor, William Craigie, he discovered that Craigie was working on the *New English Dictionary* (the original name for the *Oxford English Dictionary*, or OED). Craigie had taken over as coeditor of the project, along with C. T. Onions, after the OED's originator, James A. H. Murray, had died in 1915. The OED had originally been planned as a four-volume work that would not only define but give the history and etymologies of all words in the English language from Early Middle English forward; the first fascicle (one of the divisions of a book published in parts) was published in 1884, and by the time the entire project was completed in 1928, it had grown to twelve volumes and the language had changed so much that it was necessary to start immediately on the first supplement, for words that had entered the language in the previous forty years. Craigie offered Tolkien a job as assistant lexicographer, and in November 1918, the Tolkien family, along with Jennie Grove, took up residence at 50 St. John's Street, a short bike ride away from the dictionary offices at the Old Ashmolean. Due to the fact that most up-and-coming young linguists had been busy fighting for the past four years, work had been slow during the war. The letters U through Z still had to be completed. Tolkien was put to work in the W's, assigned the words "warm," "wasp," "water," "wick (lamp)," and "winter." In later years, when copy editors attempted to correct Tolkien's spelling of "dwarves" in *The Hobbit*, pointing out that the spelling in the OED was "dwarfs," Tolkien stood by his spelling, allegedly proclaiming, "I *wrote* the OED!" (Tolkien preferred the "dwarves" spelling as being in keeping with plurals of a more archaic origin than similar plurals that retained the "f" of the singular. He had the same objection to "elfin" rather than his own spelling, "elven.")

Since rededicating himself to his literary pursuits in the last year of the war, Tolkien had been spending an increasing amount of time on his invented languages of Quenya and Sindarin. These had ceased to be merely academic games; they had become the languages spoken by the denizens of his new world of Middle-earth. His job at the OED consisted of tracing the roots and Indo-European cognates of the English words assigned to him, a process that was very similar to the way he constructed his elvish vocabularies. Although his job was acknowledged to be somewhat tedious, it strengthened his skills as a philologist and ultimately contributed to the aura of reality that pervaded his imaginary world.

A TEACHER IS BORN

The pay at the OED was not very much, and it was assumed that the lexicographers would supplement their incomes by tutoring students enrolled at the university. Tolkien began to accumulate private students, many of them female undergraduates from Lady Margaret Hall and St. Hugh's, whose students did not have anyone available to teach Anglo-Saxon and were particularly glad to study with a married man, whose resident wife meant that they could come to his house for lessons without a chaperone. By 1920, Tolkien was earning enough from his tutoring that he could afford to move his family from their cramped flat into a proper house at 1 Alfred Street and give up his lexicography job for full-time teaching. He discovered, in fact, that he liked teaching and was good at it, conveying not only information to his students but also something of his passion for the subject. When an opening for a Reader in English Language came up at Leeds University in 1920, his old tutor Kenneth Sisam suggested he apply for it. (A Reader at a British university is a position lower in rank than a professor but higher than a tutor, roughly equivalent to an associate professor in the American university system.) The job had the additional attraction of a fairly substantial salary for the time: £500 per year, the equivalent of about $18,000 in year 2000 dollars. Although Tolkien initially did not think very much of his chances, he was asked to come for an interview in June, and by the end of the visit he knew he had the job.

Leeds was not an ancient institution like Oxford; although its roots go back to a medical school founded in 1831, the university per se was only founded in 1904. The city of Leeds itself was one of the industrial centers of northern England, in many ways the Birmingham of Yorkshire. Rather than the diverse architecture of Oxford (where Gothic-style buildings tended to be authentically Gothic), Leeds's Gothic was of strictly Victorian vintage. And once again, Tolkien was in Yorkshire while Edith was pregnant and living alone in the south. In October, just as the academic term began, Edith gave birth to the Tolkiens' second son, Michael Hilary Reuel. Tolkien shuttled back and forth between rented rooms in Leeds during the week and Oxford at the weekend, until Edith, Jennie, and the two boys were able to join him in the new year. Tolkien's ambivalence about living in the gloomy, industrial North—a part of the country he may have felt he had enough of during his recuperation during the war—led him to apply for two other jobs, one at Liverpool and one at Cape Town in South Africa. Liverpool went nowhere, but much to his surprise, he was offered the job at Cape Town. However, Edith was not in a state to travel, with a new baby, and so he passed on the offer. For once, he decided to refrain from making his own life conform to the pattern of his parents' lives. Finally, in late 1921, the Tolkiens found a small house near the university and were able to settle in.

The English department at Leeds was not only headed but essentially founded by George Gordon. He had previously taught at Oxford—although Tolkien had not really known him at the time—and he had organized the curriculum along Oxford lines, with concentrations in the literature or the linguistics of the language. Tolkien had been hired to create a syllabus for the Anglo-Saxon and Middle English course that would reach undergraduates who did not come from the linguistically sophisticated public school background that usually produced such scholars at Oxford and Cambridge. The Leeds students tended to be of a more working-class background than those at the elite universities, but Tolkien discovered that they were therefore much less likely to take their education for granted. If he could arouse an interest in philology in them, it was an authentic enthusiasm.

Now that Tolkien was committed to Leeds, he found life becoming good. Edith rather liked the social life available to her among other university wives; Leeds was not as formal as Oxford, where many dons were married to women with academic achievements of their own, a situation that Edith found intimidating. Tolkien's own social circle was also compatible. George Gordon was the kind of department head who was generous with practical assistance but knew when to let a junior colleague find his own way in learning how to teach. Then, in 1922, another colleague was added to the department: the Canadian Eric Valentine Gordon (no relation to George), whom Tolkien had tutored when he was a Rhodes scholar at Oxford. Gordon was also on the language side of the curriculum, and soon he and Tolkien had embarked on a joint project to produce a new edition of the Middle English poem *Sir Gawain and the Green Knight*.

Sir Gawain and the Green Knight was probably Tolkien's most important piece of work as an academic, becoming the standard edition of the poem and for decades many students' introduction to Middle English. *Gawain* and the poems *Pearl, Patience,* and *Cleanness* are believed to have been written by the same fourteenth-century poet, roughly of the same era as Chaucer but writing in a Midlands dialect that did not become the direct progenitor of Modern English (as Chaucer's dialect did). For this edition, Tolkien created an authoritative printed text from the single, often hard-to-decipher original, handwritten text, and compiled a glossary translating each word in the text into Modern English; Gordon wrote notes and commentary on interesting linguistic and narrative aspects of the text. Furthermore, Tolkien spent almost half a century, from the edition's publication in 1925 until his death in 1973, working on translations of *Gawain*, *Pearl*, and the Middle English poem *Sir Orfeo*, which were finally published posthumously. Aside from his epics of Middle-earth, these can be said to be the literary works that lived with him longest, were constantly in his head, and provided a subtextual backdrop to his fiction writing. Therefore, an understanding of *Gawain* and its related poems is important for understanding Tolkien's authorial mindset.

ALLITERATION AND INTERLACE

Tolkien felt a kinship with the Gawain-poet (sometimes called the Pearl-poet); literally, as the Gawain-poet is believed to have lived in the same part of the country that the Suffields later came from. It is probably also significant that, although the Gawain-poet wrote in the English language, his work shows an intimate acquaintance with the legends and tales of the nearby Welsh. Cheshire, the area where the Gawain-poet is believed to have lived, is on the border of north Wales and has a rather "Celtic" native folklore, with influences from both Wales and Ireland, the latter a direct hop across the Irish Sea. The story of Gawain and the Green Knight is an Arthurian tale, and although the European fashion for Arthuriana arose in the courts of France, Arthur himself was originally a British (i.e., Welsh) king. The French romances written by Chrétien de Troyes tended to rationalize and/or play down the fantastic elements inherited from the Breton or Welsh originals that provided their plots in favor of concentration on the etiquette and philosophy of courtly love. *Sir Gawain and the Green Knight* retains the surreal, mythological tenor of Celtic narrative tradition.

Arthur and his knights are at dinner on New Year's Day—an important holiday in the medieval calendar and a time when supernatural events were believed to be prevalent—when a gigantic green knight comes riding into the hall. He challenges any man in the hall to decapitate him, as long as he is allowed to do the same to his challenger in one year's time. Obviously, there must be a catch, but only Gawain is brave enough to take the challenge. As might be expected (at least by aficionados of medieval storytelling), the Green Knight picks up his severed head and rides off with a "See you next year!" At the appointed time, Gawain—whose reputation in Arthur's court emphasizes both his martial prowess and his courtly manners—makes his way to the Green Knight's castle, where he is entertained by the knight and his lady. Gawain and the knight agree that each day, each will give the other what he has "won" during the day, the knight while hunting, Gawain while in the castle. The wife tries her best to seduce Gawain, and each day Gawain is honor-bound to kiss the knight as his wife had kissed him (a comedy routine guaranteed to stand the test of time). However, on the last day, Gawain holds back a green belt that the lady has told him will protect him in the beheading game. When the time comes for Gawain to offer his neck as the knight had done the year before, the knight stops just short of beheading him in honor of his bravery, but nicks him just a bit for holding back the belt. It has all been a set-up to test Gawain's courage.

The motif of the beheading game appears in the Irish tale *Fled Bricrenn*, in which the challenger is the quasi-divine Cú Roí and the hero is the Irish hero par excellence Cú Chulainn. The motif also appears in the French *Livre de Carados*, a continuation of Chrétien de Troyes's Grail romance, *Perceval*, in which the hero is the Welsh/Breton Caradoc Freichfras. The motif of the severed head that continues to speak is also inescapable in both Welsh and Irish mythology. One of the interesting things about *Gawain*, then, is the way it incorporates both the very contemporary interest in Arthuriana and courtly love and the very ancient themes and semidivine characters of Celtic mythology, a mixture that is echoed in its melding of Middle English language and Welsh narrative.

Furthermore, as Tolkien points out in the introduction to his translation of the poem (published posthumously),[3] one reason that the Gawain-poet never achieved the long-lasting reputation of his contemporary, Geoffrey Chaucer, was that he chose to write in an exceedingly complicated "alliterative" style, which relies not only on rhyme but alliteration to tie the lines together: Each stanza is composed of a varying number of long lines with three alliterating stresses; each stanza then ends with one two-syllable line (called the "bob") and a trimeter quatrain (the "wheel"), rhyming *ababa*. (The other major poet of this era to use this combination of rhyme and alliteration, though not in the same pattern as is found in *Gawain*, was another Midlands man, William Langland, the author of *Piers Plowman*.) Interestingly, at the same time a poetic form called the *cywydd* (pronounced "kuh-with") was emerging in Wales, relying on the meter known as *cynghanedd* that also relies on extremely elaborate patterns of alliteration, internal rhyme, and rhyming couplets.[4] In this way, the poetry of the West Midlands around 1400 had more in common with the poetry of Wales than it did with the poetry of London, even though it shared its language with London rather than Wales.

The third section of the poem, in which Gawain is entertained at the Green Knight's castle before the beheading game, features a narrative technique known as interlace. This technique was very popular in all national literatures of the Middle Ages. The adventures of two different characters, or different sets of characters, would be related in alternating episodes in a way that compares or illustrates the story's themes; the technique echoed in narrative form the same kind of interlacing patterns found in classic medieval manuscript illuminations, where recognizably "natural" forms of men, animals, and plants were stretched and twisted to their limits until they verged on the abstract.

VIKING SONGS AND LOST TALES

Gordon was a fast worker, and while Tolkien greatly enjoyed their collaboration, he also recognized that he was working at a much quicker pace than was typical for him when working alone. It is probably no coincidence that this collaboration was also the piece of work that Tolkien completed with the least procrastination. Left to his own devices, there was always one little bit of rewriting necessary before a piece was perfect—a trait that was later to be the despair of his publishers.

Tolkien and Gordon also socialized with their students in a group called the Viking Club, which existed primarily for the consumption of vast quantities of beer and the singing of rollicking drinking songs, often composed in the Northern languages they all studied. In many ways it was like the T.C.B.S. and the Oxford dining and debating clubs that had provided Tolkien with the bulk of his school and undergraduate social life. In part, this was a natural reaction on the part of the two professors, both accustomed to this kind of highly intellectualized "hanging out" from their times at Oxford, but it also served to make them extremely popular with the students—learning Old Norse was much less of a grind when it became a kind of secret language for saying rude things about common academic enemies over several pints of beer. By 1925, Gordon and Tolkien were teaching more than a third of all English majors at Leeds; this means that linguistics students in the Leeds English department comprised a larger percentage of the total department enrollment than at Oxford. Tolkien had learned through his independent tutoring in Oxford that he enjoyed teaching; at Leeds his enjoyment was earning him a reputation as a man who could make dry, "dead" languages and literatures interesting and alive.

Academic life was more informal at Leeds than it was at Oxford, and that made Edith more comfortable. As a result, home life was calmer. In May 1923, Tolkien caught pneumonia; for his recuperation the family spent the summer near Evesham, Worcestershire, on the small farm that Hilary

Tolkien had purchased after leaving the army. Tolkien's Aunt Jane was also living in Worcestershire, at a small farm near Dormston that was known as Bag End. Tolkien continued writing poetry in his spare time; in addition to his medieval pastiches and drinking songs, he was writing poems connected to his Middle-earth mythology. One told the story of an encounter between a dragon and a "Miss Biggins"; another told of a creature with pale, glowing eyes who lived deep within the earth. Some of these poems were published that year in *Northern Ventures,* a collection of poetry by members of the Leeds English department. In addition to the poetry, Tolkien was continuing his saga proper, which he now called The Book of Lost Tales.[5] The tales relate the story of what is now considered the "First Age" of Middle-earth. Like many medieval compendia of tales (Chaucer's *Canterbury Tales* among the most famous, and Odysseus's narration of his adventures since the Trojan War to the Phaeacians, when he is washed up on their island, another cogent comparison), the history of Middle-earth is presented within a frame tale, in which a man named Eriol arrives, after a long journey, at the Lonely Isle, home of the Elves. These "lost tales" constitute the Elves' true history, narrated in response to Eriol's questions. The literary style of these tales is ornate, very reminiscent of the Victorian neo-medieval diction of William Morris's and Lord Dunsany's romances:

> And the embassy was abashed and afraid and went back unto Sirnúmen utterly cast down: yet was Manwë's heart heavier than theirs, for things had gone ill indeed, and yet he saw that worse would be; and so did the destinies of the Gods work out, for lo! to the Noldoli Manwë's words seemed cold and heartless, and they knew not his sorrow and his tenderness; and Manwë thought them strangely changed and turned to covetice, who longed but for comfort, being like children very full of the loss of their fair things.[6]

Compare this with the mock-archaic diction from a section of Morris's 1886 book *A Dream of John Ball:*

> One of them strode up to me across the road, a man some six feet high, with a short black beard and black eyes and berry-brown skin, with a huge bow in his hand bare of the case, a knife, a pouch, and a short hatchet, all clattering together at his girdle.
>   "Well, friend," said he, "thou lookest partly mazed; what tongue hast thou in thine head?"

"A tongue that can tell rhymes," said I.

"So I thought," said he. "Thirstest thou any?"

"Yea, and hunger," said I.

And therewith my hand went into my purse, and came out again with but a few small and thin silver coins with a cross stamped on each, and three pellets in each corner of the cross. The man grinned.

"Aha!" said he, "is it so? Never heed it, mate. It shall be a song for a supper this fair Sunday evening. But first, whose man art thou?"

"No one's man," said I, reddening angrily; "I am my own master."

He grinned again.

"Nay, that's not the custom of England, as one time belike it will be. Methinks thou comest from heaven down, and hast had a high place there too."[7]

Yet, although Tolkien's mythology was beginning to take a coherent form, the manuscript, in the sense of something that could be sent to a publisher in the hopes of turning it into a book, remained inchoate. Rather than pushing through to the end and then returning to edit a complete work, Tolkien would drop one story and go back to recast another, already complete in prose, as a narrative poem. Then he would skip ahead to polish another incomplete story, and then go back to something that he had thought was perfect a year ago, but now he had written something that required revision ... and on and on. His friend Christopher Wiseman had once commented that Tolkien's problem was that he could not let go of a piece of imaginative writing because then the imagining—what Tolkien later termed "sub-creation"—was over. This is a common literary dilemma, which is in part eased by the creation of series characters, but so-called genre fiction was still in its infancy and the notion of writing a number of books, all taking place within the bounds of Middle-earth, evidently did not occur to Tolkien. In the 1920s, series fiction was largely confined to murder mysteries.

YOU *CAN* GO HOME AGAIN

In 1924, Tolkien was promoted to Professor of English Language at Leeds, a position that was created specifically for him in recompense for not having been appointed Professor of English Literature two years previously, when George Gordon left Leeds to return to Oxford. This was both an academic honor and a financial blessing: Tolkien was now, at thirty-two, one of the younger full professors in Britain, and the family was able finally to buy a house. It was not a moment too soon, because Edith was once again pregnant and more room was needed. In November, the third Tolkien son, Christopher Reuel, was born. The Tolkien family seemed ready to settle down happily in Leeds: Tolkien had a good position and congenial colleagues, Edith liked the social environment, and the children had a large house surrounded by open fields in which to play. Leeds might not be as prestigious a university as Oxford or Cambridge, but there were advantages in its relative newness compared to those two ancient establishments: Tolkien was able to implement his own ideas about teaching his subject without the objections of entrenched elders who had always done it another way. He could also point to the strength of the language side of the Leeds English department and say, with complete sincerity, that this was his doing, his creation.

In June 1925, this was precisely what he did. The Rawlinson and Bosworth Professorship of Anglo-Saxon at Oxford fell vacant when its current incumbent, William Craigie, Tolkien's former boss at the *Oxford English Dictionary*, accepted a chair at the University of Chicago. This professorship was the most prestigious position in Tolkien's field, and although he felt he had little chance of getting it, he applied anyway. There was no harm in trying.

In his application letter, Tolkien was careful to detail his efforts in building up the language side of the Leeds department, noting that in a department that averaged sixty students, there had been five on the language side when he arrived in 1920, and a mere five years later there were twenty. "Philology, indeed, seems to have lost for these students its connotations of terror if not of mystery. An active discussion-class has been conducted, on lines more familiar in schools of literature than that of language ...."[8] In other words, Tolkien was not just teaching his students grammar and translation, he was teaching them to understand *Beowulf* in the same way that a student on the literature side would be taught how to interpret the plays of Shakespeare or the poetry of Milton. Tolkien listed the classes that he had taught during his five years at Leeds, and it is an impressive list: "Old English heroic verse, the history of English, various Old English and Middle English texts, Old and Middle English philology, introductory Germanic philology, Gothic, Old Icelandic (a second-year and third-year course), and Medieval Welsh."[9] Five of these he had taught just within the past year.

There were three other serious candidates for the professorship: Allen Mawer, R. W. Chambers, and Tolkien's old tutor Kenneth Sisam. Mawer ultimately decided not to apply; Chambers was offered the chair but turned it down; and the choice came down to Tolkien or Sisam. Sisam was not currently teaching—he was a senior editor at the Clarendon Press—but he was living in Oxford and still very much a presence among his former colleagues, many of whom supported his candidacy. He had a much stronger publication record than Tolkien as well, both because he had been working in the field longer and because he actually finished things. Tolkien was backed by his former head at Leeds, George Gordon, who was a master of academic politics and who was able to speak from firsthand experience of Tolkien's strengths. When it came time for the vote, the search committee was split equally. The deciding vote came down to the vice-chancellor, Joseph Wells. Swayed by Gordon's enthusiasm, he voted for Tolkien.

NOTES

1. V.H.H. Green, A History of Oxford University (London: B.T. Batsford, 1974), 188.

2. Robert Graves and Alan Hodge, The Long Weekend: A Social History of Great Britain, 1918–1939 (New York: W.W. Norton, 1940), 12.

3. J.R.R. Tolkien, trans., Sir Gawain and the Green Knight, Pearl, and Sir Orfeo (New York: Ballantine, 1975).

4. For an explanation of cynghanedd, see Rachel Bromwich's introduction to the poems, or cywyddau, of the form's most famous exponent, Dafydd ap Gwilym (Rachel Bromwich, ed. and trans., Dafydd ap Gwilym: Poems, Llandysul, Dyfed, Wales: Gomer Press, 1982).

5. These manuscripts were eventually edited and published by Christopher Tolkien as The Book of Lost Tales, Part 1 (Boston: Houghton Mifflin, 1984) and The Book of Lost Tales, Part 2 (Boston: Houghton Mifflin, 1984); they also form the preliminary basis of The Silmarillion (Boston: Houghton Mifflin, 1977).

6. Book of Lost Tales, Part 1, "The Theft of Melko," 162.

7. William Morris, A Dream of John Ball (University of Virginia Electronic Texts Center, http://etext.lib.virginia.edu/toc/modeng/public/MorDrea.html, originally published 1886) 11–13, accessed December 22, 2002.

8. Carpenter, Letters, 13.

9. Carpenter, Letters, 12.

Chapter 6

GETTING SOME INKLINGS
(1926–1932)

The Oxford to which Tolkien returned in 1926 was a far cry from the university he had entered in 1911. Indeed, the whole world had changed radically. Nonetheless, Oxford still retained its ivory-tower charm, even though an increasing number of its younger dons were veterans of the trenches of World War I. When Tolkien began his undergraduate studies, the English school was only as old as he was—it had been founded in 1893—and its program of studying "modern" literature written in English was considered a radical innovation in a curriculum previously devoted to theology, the classics, mathematics, and other timeless studies. By the time Tolkien returned to Oxford as a don, the curriculum had taken yet another step forward in offering degrees more useful for politicians, industrialists, and other denizens of the modern world: the school of Modern Greats, which studied philosophy, politics, and economics. (A proposal for an official school of science, however, was voted down in 1922, and the School of Human Sciences was not established until 1970.) Graduate and research degrees were also postwar innovations, largely introduced to accommodate foreign students and Rhodes scholars.[1] This is not to say that science or economics were not taught or studied at Oxford before this time, but that it was not possible to graduate with a degree in the subjects—in modern American terms, one could minor in these subjects but not major in them. Nonetheless, the existence of a degree in a field requires its teaching by more than one or two research professors, and official recognition of a field is a great incentive towards achievement. Oxford was also changed by the nature of its students. The hiatus of the war had created a student body that was not only chronologically more mature but, having endured the horrors of the war, also less inclined to put up with being treated as overgrown schoolboys. Political consciousness, while not as powerful a force as it was to become in the 1960s, was more prominent than it had been previously.

It was still Oxford, however, and Tolkien was happy to be back. One of his first tasks was to find a house—once again, Edith and the children had remained behind until Tolkien was ready to settle them in. He bought a house in North Oxford, at 22 Northmoor Road. North Oxford was an area that was popularly said to have sprung up virtually overnight when the university eliminated the prohibition on fellows' marriage in the 1870s. Over time, it acquired a reputation for a peculiarly Oxfordian form of dowdy eccentricity as it developed a population of stereotypically unworldly dons, their wives often more educated in history than in housekeeping, spinster ladies with interests in vegetarianism and Theosophy, and a general tendency towards "good works and earnest discussion," as one writer puts it.[2] It is not in the least out of character that the international charity Oxfam was founded in North Oxford in 1942.

The new Tolkien abode was about a mile north of the university, and Tolkien usually biked to classes. His classes were mostly held in the Examination Schools building, just east of Merton College. The organization of Oxford University is such that chairs such as the Rawlinson and Bosworth Chair were university positions, but the university as a physical entity does not actually exist; the buildings where the tasks of teaching, research, and infighting took place all belonged to the colleges, which were separate organizational entities. Thus, professors such as Tolkien had to be nominally assigned to a specific college, although the professor was not a member of the college in the same way that its fellows were—fellows were elected by the college itself, while professors were more or less wished on them. Therefore, there was always a chance that a professor would be resented within his college, and it took a certain amount of personal charm and politicking to achieve a comfortable fit. Tolkien's professorship was located in Pembroke College, and that is where he was expected to attend college dinners, socialize in the Senior Common Room, and partake in all the other activities of an Oxford don.

THE LIFE OF AN OXFORD DON

The terms of Tolkien's chair required him to deliver at least thirty-six lectures per year on the topics of Anglo-Saxon and Middle English. In reality, he usually delivered between 72 and 136 lectures per year in order to give the topic what he felt was its due. His students also felt that he gave the topic its due: Many retained lifelong memories of Tolkien striding into a lecture hall, slamming down his books on the lectern, and bellowing the opening lines of *Beowulf:*

Hwæt! We Gardena in geardagum,
þeodcyninga, þrym gefrunon,
hu ða æþelingas ellen fremedon.[3]

One of his students, J. I. M. Stewart (who became an Oxford don himself and wrote murder mysteries under the name of Michael Innes), recalled that "He could turn a lecture room into a mead hall in which he was the bard and we were the feasting, listening guests."[4]

Most of Tolkien's time was spent in preparing his lectures, a task he undertook with his usual perfectionist attention to detail as well as his usual propensity for abandoning a project in midstream when he was not able to complete it to his satisfaction. He was also expected to oversee the research of postgraduate students. Although his chair was extremely prestigious, the pay was not sufficient to support a family of five—six after the birth of the Tolkiens' final child, daughter Priscilla Mary Reuel, in 1929—in total comfort. Tolkien earned extra money by serving as an external examiner at other universities in Britain and Ireland and by marking School Certificates (the exam taken by those leaving secondary school). Although many of his colleagues were in later years inclined to blame his rather meager record of scholarly publication (he never produced an entire monograph on any aspect of Anglo-Saxon or Middle English; all his publications were articles or editions of texts) on the amount of time he "wasted" writing his unforgivably popular fantasies, at least as much blame should probably be laid on the amount of time he spent marking exams.

AN ACADEMIC CRUSADE

Tolkien, fresh from his success in devising a language curriculum at Leeds, returned to Oxford full of ideas about revising the English curriculum there as well. There was little leeway in choosing one's classes at Oxford in the early twentieth century, infinitely less than there is in contemporary American higher education. To a great extent, this was the result of the standard examinations that everyone who took a degree in English had to pass—one did not take finals in a specific class at the end of a term, but took an overall examination at the end of one's entire course of study. The school was called the School of English Language and

Literature, and true to its name, it offered a degree with equal emphasis on language—linguistics, philology, the history of the English language—and literature from *Beowulf* to Wordsworth, almost all of it poetry (except, of course, for Shakespeare). Since the interests of the two sides did not often overlap, the linguists spent a lot of time reading literature that bored them to tears, and the literary critics learned far more than they ever wanted to know about the declension of the verb *weorþan*. Partly this was because it was felt that an English graduate should be well versed in all aspects of the topic, but partly it was the result of academic power struggles—every professor wants all the students to study his own area of expertise, because after all, if it were not the most important aspect of the curriculum, why would he have bothered to specialize in it?

Tolkien had two goals in his proposed revision of the curriculum—he wanted to allow students more leeway in their choice of classes in their final year, so that each could devote time to their real area of interest, and he wanted to refocus the linguistics classes so that there was as much emphasis on understanding the medieval works as works of art as there was in understanding the operation of Anglo-Saxon grammar and etymology. (Somewhat ironically, Tolkien's plans for the linguistics side would have the effect of making those classes rather more attractive to the more literarily inclined.) Although this scheme seems rather self-evident given the eventual development of university curricula over the next fifty years, it was almost universally dismissed by his colleagues when Tolkien first began airing the subject. It was necessary for the entire English faculty to approve any change to the curriculum, and it took six years for Tolkien to muster enough support for his program. Yet with quiet persistence and masterful networking (he had evidently learned much about academic politics from George Gordon during his years at Leeds), he succeeded. The *Handbook to the University of Oxford* for 1932 outlines the new curriculum, perhaps Tolkien's greatest contribution to the teaching of English in that its effects reached far beyond himself and his own field: "The School," it noted "has recently been rearranged so as to give a choice between three Courses. In all the Courses students are expected to have some knowledge of the history of the language, and in the historical background, but in Courses I and II stress is laid on the earlier literature, and in Course III on more modern literature."[5] Course I focused on medieval literature and philology; students who chose this course could also study the languages and literatures of Gothic, Old Saxon, Old or Middle High German, Old Norse, or Old French. Course II was also medieval and early modern in focus but only concentrated on works in the English language up to the times of Shakespeare, Spenser, and Milton. Course III covered English literature including Old and Middle English but focused on the later literature, especially Chaucer, Spenser, Shakespeare, Donne, Milton, Dryden, Pope, Johnson, and Wordsworth. The handbook noted that Course III "will be found a good preparation for those who contemplate a literary life."[6]

"NEVER TRUST A PAPIST OR A PHILOLOGIST"

In the course of his lobbying for curriculum change, Tolkien became acquainted with another of the English faculty, the new Fellow and Tutor in English Language and Literature of Magdalen College, Clive Staples "Jack" Lewis, who had also started teaching at Oxford in 1925. Although both were medievalists, they did not hit it off very well at first. Lewis was initially opposed to Tolkien's vision of a new curriculum, belonging to the "literature" side of the school and therefore uninterested in any proposal offered by the "language" opposition. In his autobiography, Lewis recalled that "At my first coming into the world, I had been (implicitly) warned never to trust a Papist, and at my first coming into the English faculty (explicitly) never to trust a philologist. Tolkien was both."[7]

Lewis was Irish, son of a Belfast lawyer. Like Tolkien, he had lost his mother when he was a child—she died of cancer when he was nine—and he had one brother—Warren, known as Warnie, who was three years his elder. After his mother's death, Jack had been sent to public school in England, first to Wynyard School in Hertfordshire, where the headmaster was slowly going insane and daily life included bad teaching, bad sanitation, bad food, and a reign of terror featuring arbitrary beatings. At fourteen he won a scholarship to Malvern College, a much more stable environment, but Lewis had already conceived a not unnatural loathing of boarding schools and convinced his father to send him to a private tutor instead. His new teacher, W. T. Kirkpatrick, had been the headmaster of Lewis Senior's old school; he was a ruthlessly logical intellect as well as an atheist, two habits of mind that Lewis found increasingly attractive. He had already found himself slipping away from a belief in a benevolent God as a result of overwhelming evidence to the contrary; his training in logical investigation led him to regard Christianity as merely one mythology among many, no more real than Germanic paganism and based on a holy text whose literary style was considerably less enthralling. Lewis was a voracious reader and found himself most drawn to what he and his friend Arthur Greeves called "Northernness": Norse mythology, Wagner's *Ring* cycle, and the romances of William Morris.

Lewis had entered University College, Oxford, in 1916—just as Tolkien left the university—and his education was almost immediately interrupted when he was called up in 1917. Although he found war appalling, as far as he was concerned it failed to surpass the horrors of public school. During training he was billeted with another Irishman, Edward Francis Courtney Moore, known as Paddy. Moore's mother, Mrs. Janie Moore, and his sister, Maureen, took rooms in Oxford to be near him while he was in training. Mrs. Moore was separated from her husband, Paddy's father, whom she usually referred to as "the Beast." For some reason, the resolutely logical and nonspiritual Lewis, aged nineteen, found himself getting along like a house on fire with a forty-five-year-old, poorly educated, intellectually unfocussed woman. When he and Paddy left for the trenches, they each promised the other that, should something happen to one of them, the survivor would look after the other's parent. Paddy was killed in 1918, and Lewis publicly claimed, over the ensuing thirty-five years, that the reason he lived with Mrs. Moore was merely the fulfillment of his wartime vow to his comrade. The fact of the matter was, however, that they were almost certainly lovers, emotionally if not physically.

When Lewis returned to Oxford to complete his studies, Mrs. Moore came with him; despite the fact that he had rooms in his college like all the other undergraduates, he spent most of his time at the house that the two of them rented together. In 1922, he earned a first-class degree in Greats—classics, ancient history, and philosophy—but since there did not seem to be any chance of a teaching position in philosophy, he decided to study for an additional degree in English Language and Literature, earning the degree—first class again—in one year rather than the usual three. He tended to look down on the intellectual caliber of the English department in comparison to classics, however, and he increasingly disliked modern literature, with its ironic, cynical, disillusioned attitude born in the trenches of World War I. After finishing his second degree, he spent a year or so living on an allowance from his father, picking up an occasional teaching job, and applying for whatever positions came open. In 1925, he finally was elected a fellow in English at Magdalen College.

Lewis was brash and decided in his beliefs—perhaps having been trained to think logically and to derive his positions from facts rather than feelings, he was inclined to believe that he was innately right, and those who disagreed with him simply had not thought things through to a sufficient degree. For Lewis, one started with facts and worked forward to an opinion. Tolkien, in contrast, was much more low-key in expressing his opinions, more inclined to win people to his point of view by simply talking about his ideas until they soaked into his opponents' consciousness by osmosis and, more significantly, arrived at his insights in flashes of inspiration and then worked backward until he had discovered their foundation. His intuitive approach to scholarship was part of the reason he was such an exceptional philologist, since the methodology of philology requires one to start with something that is attested at one point in time and must have evolved to get there, but whose previous forms are unknown. Philological reconstruction requires the same kind of retrospective intuition that Tolkien excelled at, and which he applied to his invented languages as well. Lewis was not a philologist; Tolkien remarked that Lewis had a "curious ability … to misunderstand etymology."[8]

COALBITERS AND COMRADES

Despite, or perhaps because of, the differences in their temperaments, their mutual love of "Northernness" soon drew the two together. Lewis began attending an informal seminar in Old Icelandic that Tolkien organized, the Coalbiters. (The name came from the Icelandic word *kolbítar*, "those who sit so close to the fire that they bite the coal"—a cozy and intimate group.) Part of Tolkien's proposal for the revised English curriculum was a greater prominence for Old Icelandic in the philological track, and his ploy for introducing waverers and doubters to the joys of reading the Norse legends and sagas as literature was to show them the texts in all their glory. The group's original members already had some experience with Old Icelandic—R. M. Dawkins, the professor of Byzantine and modern Greek; C. T. Onions, the editor of the *Oxford English Dictionary* and one of Tolkien's former bosses on that project; G. E. K. Braunholtz, the professor of comparative philology; and John Fraser, the professor of Celtic. However, other members included Old Icelandic neophytes George Gordon, John Bryson of Balliol, the historian Bruce McFarlane, and Nevill Coghill, a fellow at Exeter College who had been a close friend with Lewis when they were both undergraduates. Gordon, Bryson, and Coghill were all friends with Lewis and one or all of them may have encouraged him to join the group. In any case, by January 1927, Lewis was sitting in on the translation sessions. Although each member would work on reading the set text on his own in between sessions, taking the time to look up unfamiliar words and working out difficult grammatical constructions, in the actual meetings, everyone was expected to take his turn translating by sight. Tolkien could whip through a dozen pages with fluency; those with some previous knowledge could manage a page or so before breaking down; the neophytes would struggle through maybe a paragraph at a time, with the occasional hand from Tolkien. It was in the course of these translation sessions, which lasted some six or seven years as the group worked their way through the sagas and the Eddas, that Lewis and Tolkien grew to realize that they shared an emotional response to the texts that went beyond linguistics or literature and resided in myth.

As Tolkien settled into life at Oxford, he began to miss the close male friendships that he had enjoyed with the T.C.B.S. at school and throughout college and the army, and with Eric Gordon at Leeds. Edith did not like the social life at Oxford any better than she had before Leeds, and so Tolkien's own existence was once more dichotomized into his private family life, revolving around wife and children, and his public academic life, which was almost entirely masculine. Yet although the company of his fellow dons at High Table, in the Senior Common Room, and in the Coalbiters provided him an intellectual outlet and his relationships with Edith and the children sustained his emotional life, he missed the artistic fellowship that he had shared with Smith, Gilson, and Wiseman. Sadly, though Christopher Wiseman had survived the war and Tolkien had even named his third son after him, as their lives had taken different paths, that boyhood closeness had became attenuated. Tolkien was continuing to write poems, most of them deriving from his Middle-earth mythology and some of them recastings in poetic form of the stories in his Book of Lost Tales. However, he was starving for feedback. After three years of Icelandic translation and a long late-night conversation on the giants and gods of Asgard, Tolkien finally gathered up the courage to show his still-unfinished poem "The Gest of Beren and Lúthien" to Lewis in December 1929.

Lewis was enchanted by the poem and the invented mythology of Middle-earth that lay behind it. That did not stop him from presenting Tolkien with a thorough critique of the lines he thought weak, however. Perhaps to soften the blows of criticism, he presented his critique in the form of a "scholarly commentary" on the poem as though it were an authentic medieval text, suggesting that infelicities were the result of the scribal errors and the other mishaps that manuscripts are heir to. Tolkien's response was typical of his reactions to critique; he rewrote the poem from top to bottom, rarely adopting Lewis's suggestions verbatim (and indeed, most of Lewis's suggested rewrites completely missed the mark of Tolkien's vision), but reworking all the sections that Lewis had identified as weak. In a letter to Charles Moorman, written in 1959, Lewis commented that "No-one ever influenced Tolkien; you might as well try to influence a bandersnatch."[9] Yet Lewis's conception of "influence" seems to be itself heavily shaped by his own assumptions of logical rightness; Tolkien may not have agreed with the precise solutions that Lewis proposed for his works, but he did recognize that Lewis could pinpoint his weaknesses and he especially appreciated Lewis's encouragement. Soon he was reading Lewis longer and longer extracts of his Silmarillion.

Others also emerged to offer advice and encouragement. As the Coalbiters reached the end of the corpus of Old Icelandic texts and ceased to meet, Lewis and Tolkien began attending meetings of a club organized by an extremely literary undergraduate named Edward Tangye Lean. The Inklings, as they were called, consisted of both undergraduates and dons; they would read literary works-in-progress out loud and receive the comments of the rest of the club. When Tangye Lean left the university in 1933 the club in its original format fell apart, but Lewis and Tolkien continued to meet on a more or less weekly basis, along with a coterie of likeminded adults (the undergraduate element was not replicated until Christopher Tolkien entered the university in the 1940s), and they maintained the habit of calling themselves Inklings.

THE INKLINGS

Most of the core members of the Inklings were Lewis's friends, many of them dating from his undergraduate days. Chief among them was Warnie Lewis, Jack's brother; a retired army captain, he lived with his brother and Mrs. Moore at the Kilns, their home in North Oxford. Owen Barfield had worked as a journalist after taking his degree, until the necessity of providing for a wife and children forced him, in 1931, to enter his father's legal practice. Humphrey Havard was a medical doctor, the family doctor of both the Tolkien and Lewis households. Hugo Dyson was a lecturer in English at Reading University and often lectured at the Oxford University Extension. Charles Williams, an editor for the Oxford University Press, was the odd man out in the group; he was neither an academic nor did he have a university degree. He was a man of an unusually mystical bent, an initiate of the Order of the Golden Dawn (a fellowship devoted to the practice of ritual magic that numbered, at various times, both the poet W. B. Yeats and the mage Aleister Crowley—the self-proclaimed "wickedest man in the world"—among its members), and was fascinated with both Christianity and the occult.

Williams had published several novels that he termed "occult thrillers" in the early 1930s, before he became acquainted with the Inklings: *War in Heaven* (1930), *Many Dimensions* (1931), *The Place of the Lion* (1931), *The Greater Trumps* (1932), and *Shadows of Ecstasy* (1933). Williams's novels took place in the present and involved a type of supernatural mystery/adventure in which a graduate student writing her dissertation might find herself confronted with true Platonic Ideals breaking through into mundane reality, or an archdeacon, a duke, and an editor find themselves on a quest for the Holy Grail—books that really fit into no recognizable genre until the advent of *The X Files* in the 1990s. His novels were never bestsellers—indeed, it was a long while before he could get them published at all—but they came to the attention of some of the Inklings, such as Nevill Coghill and R. W. Chambers, and thus to Jack Lewis. He was enchanted by *The Place of the Lion* and in March 1936, wrote an enthusiastic letter of appreciation to Williams, who himself had just proofread the galleys of Lewis's *The Allegory of Love* as part of his duties at the Oxford University Press and was similarly enthralled. The two began corresponding and when Williams, along with the rest of the press, was evacuated from London to Oxford in 1939, Lewis invited him to sit in on the Inklings gatherings.

CONVERTING LEWIS

Lewis had undergone a slow but fervent reconversion to Christianity throughout the 1920s. His undergraduate study of philosophy had led him from a position of atheism to agnosticism. He found it necessary, as a philosopher, to posit some kind of Hegelian Absolute Mind underlying the universe, but he regarded the theology and trappings of Christianity as "childish superstition." Nonetheless, the people he was closest to— Tolkien, Coghill, Barfield, his childhood friend and lifelong correspondent Arthur Greeves—were all religious men, and the writers he most respected—Thomas Malory, Edmund Spenser, John Milton, John Donne—were devout men whose works could not be understood without reference to Christian theology. Between 1926 and 1929 he began to accept the existence of God and the experience of the supernatural, but he still did not see the relevance of Christ, and he still regarded "myth" as the equivalent of "fairy tale": potentially moving, but ultimately fictional.

On the night of September 19, 1931, Lewis invited Tolkien and Hugo Dyson to have dinner with him. After the meal, the three strolled through the grounds of Magdalen College and along Addison's Walk discussing myth and metaphor. Lewis persisted in regarding myth, like metaphor, as being at one step removed from reality, and as being creations of the human mind and human speech, not creations of God. But Tolkien argued that if Man is the creation of God, then whatever Man creates— whether abstract thought or mythic narrative—is also the creation of God, even if it is only an imperfect version of God's creation—a sub-creation, as Tolkien termed it. Recalling the conversation about a month later in a letter to Arthur Greeves, Lewis reconstructed the argument:

Now what Tolkien and Dyson showed me was this: that if I met the idea of sacrifice in a Pagan story I didn't mind it at all: again, that if I met the idea of a god sacrificing himself to himself ... I liked it very much and was mysteriously moved by it: again, that idea of the dying and reviving god (Balder, Adonis, Bacchus) similarly moved me provided I met it anywhere *except* in the Gospels. The reason was that in Pagan stories I was prepared to feel the myth as profound and suggestive of meanings beyond my grasp even tho' I could not say in cold prose "what it meant."

Now the story of Christ is simply a true myth: a myth working on us in the same way as the others, but with this tremendous difference that *it really happened*: and one must be content to accept it in the same way, remembering that it is God's myth where the others are men's myths: i.e., the Pagan stories are God expressing Himself through the mind of poets, using such images as He found there, while Christianity is God expressing himself through what we call "real things."[10]

This understanding of the reality of myth, which led to Lewis returning to Christianity, was the understanding that informed not only Tolkien's own faith, but also his literary philosophy. While he could never dream of creating a myth as real as God's creation of Christ, his myth of Middle-earth was a sub-creation that still presented, if palely, God's truth and God's reality.

The years leading up to Lewis's return to Christianity were probably the phase when he and Tolkien were closest. They were agreed on their beliefs about art, and for Tolkien, art and faith were indissolubly intertwined. When Lewis returned to religion, Tolkien hoped that he would return to what, for Tolkien, was the true religion, the best expression of Christianity: Catholicism. Lewis, however, gave his allegiance to the Anglican church. For Tolkien, this seems in many ways to have been the religious equivalent of Lewis's inexplicable (to him) unsoundness in etymology, or his tone-deaf emendations of Tolkien's neo-Gothic poetic diction into eighteenth-century epigrammatic couplets. It was a kind of cognitive dissonance that widened over the years into an unspoken estrangement. However, in 1931, Lewis's conversion merely marked a shift in socializing, as the private friendship between the two men widened to encompass the larger group of the Inklings.

Warnie Lewis recalled a typical meeting of the group in a memoir he wrote to accompany the publication of his brother's letters:

> ... We met in Jack's rooms at Magdalen every Thursday evening after dinner. Proceedings neither began nor terminated at any fixed hour, though there was a tacit agreement that ten-thirty was as late as one could decently arrive.... The ritual of an Inklings was unvarying. When half a dozen or so had arrived, tea would be produced, and then when pipes were well alight Jack would say, "Well, has nobody got anything to read us?" Out would come a manuscript, and we would settle down to sit in judgement upon it—real unbiased judgement, too, since we were no mutual admiration society: praise for good work was unstinted, but censure for bad work—or even not-so-good-work—was often brutally frank.[11]

In addition to the Thursday evening meetings, many of the Inklings also congregated on Tuesdays in the pub called the Eagle and Child, or more colloquially the Bird and Baby. Those meetings were devoted more to talk—and drinking beer—than reading manuscripts. In many ways, Tolkien was reverting completely to a form that had been established with the original T.C.B.S. and continued with the Viking Club at Leeds: a bunch of chaps eating, drinking, and making merry, which in their case meant making highly abstruse jokes about incredibly esoteric subjects. By the mid-1940s, the gatherings at the Bird and Baby were such a fixture of Oxford life that they became a bit of local color in murder mysteries: In Edmund Crispin's second novel featuring the Oxford don/detective Gervase Fen (himself supposed to be the Professor of English Language and Literature), Fen, sitting in the Bird and Baby, comments, "There goes C.S. Lewis—it must be Tuesday."[12]

NOTES

1. Green, A History of Oxford University, 178–179.

2. David Horan, Oxford: A Cultural and Literary Companion (Northampton, Mass.: Interlink Books, 2000), 220.

3. Beowulf, http://www.georgetown.edu/labyrinth/library/oe/texts/a4.1.html, accessed December 22, 2002.

4. Philip Norman, "The Prevalence of Hobbits." The New York Times Magazine (January 15, 1967), 101.

5. Handbook to the University of Oxford (Oxford: Clarendon Press, 1932), 157.

6. Ibid., 158.

7. C.S. Lewis, Surprised by Joy: The Shape of My Early Life (London: William Collins, 1955), 173.

8. A.N. Wilson, *C.S. Lewis: A Biography* (London: Collins, 1990), 276–77.

9. *Letters of C.S. Lewis*, 481.

10. Walter Hooper, ed., *They Stand Together: The Letters of C.S. Lewis to Arthur Greeves (1914–1963)* (London: Collins, 1979), 427.

11. *Letters of C.S. Lewis*, 33–34.

12. Edmund Crispin, *Swan Song* (London: Walker, 1947; Avon reprint 1981), 62.

J.R.R. Tolkien, portait from 1967. © AP Photo

J.R.R. Tolkien, reading in his study, 1955. © Hulton/Archive

A still from the 2001 film The Fellowship of the Ring, picturing Elijah Wood as Frodo Baggins at Rivendale. © The Kobol Collection / New Line / Saul Zaentz / Wing Nut

Chapter 7

LIFE IN A HOBBIT HOLE
(1933–1937)

For Tolkien, "real" writing was his poetry and his myths of Middle-earth. After all, when the T.C.B.S. had their last get-together before they all went off to war, they had not vowed to follow in the footsteps of Charles Dickens or Jane Austen. In the early twentieth century, poetry was still the most prestigious form of creative writing, expressing timeless truths and reflecting the deep realities of life. Novels were literally superficial—concerned with the surface of things—exploring the intricacies of social life and personal relationships. Genre novels were even more lightweight, entertainment rather than art.

However, Tolkien's beliefs about art and literature did not prevent him from appreciating a good story on its own terms. One of his delights was making up stories to tell to his children. Some of his stories were inspired simply by aspects of the surrounding environment: A long-running family epic revolved around the tireless efforts of Major Road Ahead to prosecute the villain Bill Stickers, inspired by signs hanging on various Oxford gates. On a summer trip to the beach, Tolkien soothed his son Michael after the loss of a toy dog with the adventures of a dog named Rover, turned into a toy after annoying a wizard, who is lost on a beach by his boy and then found by the sand-sorcerer Psamathos Psamathides. The sorcerer gives Rover the power to move and sends him to the Moon, where he encounters the White Dragon and has other doggie adventures. This story was popular enough with the children that Tolkien wrote it up; it was eventually published long after Tolkien's death, although his publisher was never interested in it during his lifetime.

Another popular character within the family was Tom Bombadil, based on a Dutch doll belonging to Michael. (Michael's toys seemed to be a fertile field for story characters in the Tolkien home.) Although Tolkien apparently told many ephemeral, spur-of-the-moment tales about Tom, his initial efforts to write them down went nowhere. The first stories set Tom's adventures in the reign of King Bonhedig, and from the very beginning Tom was an ancient but active being. In 1934, Tolkien published a poem in the *Oxford Magazine* about Tom, in which Tom meets Goldberry, daughter of the River-woman; Old Man Willow, who traps him within a crack in his trunk; and a Barrow Wight, a ghost from one of the neolithic burial mounds that dotted the Berkshire Downs outside of Oxford. The elements of the Bombadil stories suggest that Tolkien was playing with Welsh folklore and mythology as he made them up: *Bonhedig*, for instance, is a Welsh word meaning "noble" or "well-born"; Celtic mythology is full of river goddesses (such as Sabrina, goddess of the Severn; Shannon, goddess of the Shannon; Sequanna, goddess of the Seine; Deva, goddess of the Dee; and the highly important goddess Danu, mother of Irish and Welsh gods, whose name persists in the Danube and Don rivers). Sacred trees, usually connected with death, are found from Iron Age Celtic archaeological sites on the Continent through medieval Irish stories; and throughout the Celtic realms, barrows and burial mounds are the abodes of gods, fairies, banshees, and pookas—supernatural beings who are not generally well disposed towards humans. Tom himself, as the most ancient one with a sense of humor, bears some resemblance to the Irish deity the Dagda ("Good Father"), suitably bowdlerized for children. (The Dagda in his natural environment is decidedly R-rated.) Tolkien regarded Tom as the spirit of the vanishing countryside; after the success of *The Lord of the Rings*, Tolkien published a collection of poems called *The Adventures of Tom Bombadil* (1962), which included several poems about the character, at the request of his Aunt Jane. The family popularity of Tolkien's stories was not confined to the children.

In 1932, Tolkien purchased an automobile: a Morris Crowley. The car was called "Jo" after the first two letters of its license plate, and Tolkien had a tendency to drive it like a knight on his prancing charger. On the family's first long-distance road trip, to visit Hilary Tolkien on his Evesham fruit farm, the car's tires punctured twice (a rather common hazard of the time) and Tolkien managed to knock down a stone wall near Chipping Norton (for which he had no one to blame but himself). Tolkien's technique for navigating busy intersections was to ignore all other vehicles and floor it, yelling "Charge'em and they scatter!" as he blasted his way through traffic.[1] While Tolkien apparently modeled himself as a driver after Mr. Toad of Toad Hall in Kenneth Grahame's *The Wind in the Willows* (1908), Edith took the more circumspect approach of Ratty and Mole and refused to get in a car with him. Tolkien decided to give up owning a car at the beginning of World War II, influenced by a combination of petrol-rationing and an awareness of the damage that automobile traffic was causing to the countryside. Nonetheless, he was inspired by his automotive adventures to write a story called "Mr. Bliss," about a man who buys a bright yellow automobile for five shillings and embarks on a series of misadventures on a drive accompanied by his neighbors: some bears, dogs, and a donkey. However, they leave behind the girabbit, a rabbit with a long, giraffelike neck. Cars prove to be an expensive proposition, not least due to the number of collisions Mr. Bliss gets into, and in the end he decides that he does not like cars very much. The original manuscript was beautifully illustrated by Tolkien, which ultimately made it too expensive to produce when he first offered it to his publishers after the success of *The Hobbit*. However, the book did eventually join the ranks of Tolkien's posthumous publications.

Tolkien's delight in illustration was also evident in the letters he wrote to his children each year, ostensibly from Father Christmas. The letters, like many holiday greetings, caught the children up on Father Christmas's doings over the past year, which often involved mishaps that threatened the production and distribution of presents. Sometimes Father Christmas was too busy or ill to write much, so his secretary, the elf Ilbereth, would take over his correspondence. Many included drawings, like snapshots, of the events in the letter. One of the longer letters, from 1932, tells of Polar Bear getting lost in underground caves, where he arouses the enmity of the goblins who live there. The cave walls are covered with paintings like those of the Paleolithic caves at Altamira, Spain (the caves at Lascaux, which are today more famous, were not discovered until 1940). The goblins retaliate by stealing all of the presents in Father Christmas's storehouse by means of a tunnel they have been burrowing out through the rock, but Father Christmas smokes them out with his "patent green luminous smoke," and the Red Gnomes capture the goblins as they flood through the other end of the tunnel.[2]

Tolkien's family stories were lighthearted entertainments, but he took them seriously enough to write many of them down. Some of the stories may have been written down because they were such favorites, while others, such as Tom Bombadil, survived by being translated into poetry. In some cases, the writing was an excuse for illustration, a talent that Tolkien enjoyed using in private although he never considered himself of professional caliber. He began to draw pictures illustrating his Silmarillion stories to concretize his mental images, especially of his mythic landscapes. He also enjoyed drawing maps of his fictional worlds, which not only helped him visualize their geography but also helped him work out practical matters like how long it would take to travel from point A to point B.

UNMODERN LITERATURE

In an interview in 1968, Tolkien claimed not to like modern literature.[3] He admitted that he had "not been nurtured by English Literature ... for the simple reason that I have never found much there in which to rest my heart (or heart and head together)."[4] However, he also admitted to reading a lot of science fiction and fantasy. Tolkien's definition of "modern literature" seems to have been limited to what today is termed "literary fiction," the highbrow stuff based in modernism. This literary movement, a postwar reaction against the realism of Victorian literature, is exemplified by the poetry of T. S. Eliot and the novels of James Joyce: fragmented, ironic, allusive, and "difficult." It was based more on psychology, which at the time was almost purely Freudian, than on philosophy; its archetypal narrative mode was stream-of-consciousness. As modernism spread, the kind of poetry that Tolkien (and Lewis) wrote became increasingly old-fashioned—no one did meter any more!—and the kind of coherent, plot-driven narrative that he valued became increasingly relegated to genre fiction and children's literature.

Lewis and Tolkien decided that since the kind of literature they liked to read was not being written (or at least not being published), they would have to write it themselves. Since plot was now the province of genre fiction, they decided to write science fiction, with Lewis taking the theme of space travel and Tolkien the theme of time travel. However, despite the genre label, they agreed that the ultimate goal of their tales would be the discovery of myth which, of course, they both agreed was ultimately the truth of religion. Lewis's story turned into *Out of the Silent Planet* (1938), the first of his trilogy about the philologist Ransom (in some ways a Lewisification of Tolkien) and his battles against the machinations of the evil physicist Weston; it was followed by *Perelandra* (1943) and *That Hideous Strength* (1945). Tolkien's story, called The Lost Road,[5] was yet another of his abortive projects; it was outlined as a series of episodes taking place at several different points in historical time—the twentieth century, Anglo-Saxon England, and Lombard Germany—and in mythic time—Ireland of the Túatha Dé Danaan, and in the Middle-earth eras of Beleriand and of the Fall of Númenor. This was one of his first efforts to use his Middle-earth mythology in the context of a modern novel. The stories he had written as part of The Book of Lost Tales were cast as authentic "ancient" narratives, echoing the oral narrative style of Beowulf or the Eddas. This type of narrative is long on action and dialogue, but does not delve very deeply into the psychology of its characters. Motivation is social and external, and emotions are expressed by people announcing what they are feeling. With The Lost Road, Tolkien begins experimenting with more modern narrative techniques, especially the use of interior monologue.

Of all Tolkien's stories, however, the one that most took on a life of its own concerned the adventures of the hobbit Bilbo Baggins. The precise date of Tolkien's inspiration is uncertain, although he knew it took place after the family moved from 22 Northmoor Road to the more spacious house next door, No. 20, at the end of 1929. It happened one summer day as he was grading School Certificate exams, and he found an empty page at the end of an exam book. Without thinking much about it, he wrote the sentence, "In a hole in the ground there lived a hobbit." Then his philological instincts kicked in, and he realized that he needed to find out what hobbits were.

One children's book that was very popular in the Tolkien household (so much so that Michael later tried to write more stories about it) was called The Marvellous Land of the Snergs, by E. A. Wyke-Smith (1927). Snergs were a race of small beings, humanlike but only about the height of a table, of stocky build and great strength. The story concerned a pair of children embarking on an adventurous journey under the guidance of a Snerg named Gorbo. The quest format and the humor of the story, as well as the general stature and social organization of the Snergs, seem to have been a strong influence on the invention of the hobbits. Another influence, somewhat more surprising given Tolkien's avowed dislike of modern literature and especially "funny" novels, was Sinclair Lewis's social satire Babbitt (1922), the story of a self-satisfied, middle-class Midwesterner who comes to question the mindless conformity of his life as a prosperous real-estate agent, breaks out, briefly, into a wild Bohemian phase, but finally returns to his comfortable fold, externally conventional, but inwardly changed. The consonance of "Babbitt" and "hobbit" suggested to Tolkien the smugness of hobbit life, out of which Bilbo is shaken by his adventure with the dwarves; also like Babbitt, he returned to his old style of life, regaining his social status after his "Bohemian" adventure, but inwardly changed forever. The similarity between Babbitt and Bilbo extended when Tolkien came to write his "new hobbit" sequel: Babbitt ends by secretly approving of his son's elopement, a break for freedom that he himself is incapable of achieving, and Bilbo passes the torch—or Ring—to his nephew Frodo, who may be able to achieve the quest that Bilbo is not called to.

After the arrival of the word "hobbit," the concept brewed in Tolkien's subconscious and melded with some of the bedtime stories he told to the boys. He constructed Thror's map. The story originally took place in its own world, a never-never fairy-tale land of dwarves and dragons. However, even though "hobbits" had never been part of The Silmarillion, the story evolved until it was recognizably taking place in some forgotten corner of Middle-earth. (Tolkien's later references throughout *The Lord of the Rings* to the lack of knowledge about hobbits among the other peoples of Middle-earth seem to be an in-joke about this late arrival to the mythology.)

THE ADVENTURES OF BILBO THE BURGLAR

The Hobbit is a story of hobbits, dwarves, men, elves, orcs, wargs, and wizards. Like many fairy tales, it follows a rather simple quest tale: the dwarf Thorin Oakenshield wants to recover the homeland and treasure stolen from his people by the dragon Smaug. He has assembled a group of dwarves (Dwalin and Balin, Fíli and Kíli, Dori, Nori, and Ori, Óin and Glóin, Bifur, Bofur, and Bombur—all names taken from a list of dwarves in the *Elder Edda*) to accompany him to the Lonely Mountain, but the company numbers an unpropitious thirteen. Furthermore, the dwarves agree that it would be wise to include in their part a professional in matters of the "recovery" of goods: a burglar. The wizard Gandalf (a name from the same Eddic source), a figure who travels easily among all the various races of (Middle-)earth, provides them with Bilbo Baggins, a most respectable and highly adventure-averse hobbit. The staid, stay-at-home side of Bilbo is appalled at the idea, but his deeply hidden adventurous side is secretly excited at the prospect.

Bilbo finds himself, willy-nilly, on an adventure. The first part of the journey takes the band from the Shire, home of the hobbits, to Mirkwood. Gandalf accompanies them on parts of the journey, but Bilbo is left to prove himself to the dwarves. The journey starts out unfavorably, with the party captured by a trio of trolls. They are rescued by Gandalf, who diverts the trolls into fighting amongst themselves (by means of trick voices) until they are caught by the rising sun, which turns them to stone.

This episode establishes a recurring pattern of dwarfish behavior: They never turn up in a complete group. For instance, when the dwarves show up at Bilbo's doorstep, Dwalin arrives alone, followed by Balin. Kíli and Fíli arrive together, followed by Dori, Nori, Ori, Óin, and Glóin. Finally

Bifur, Bofur, Bombur, and Thorin arrive. (Even when it comes to names, dwarves tend to come in sets of twos or threes, except for the leader who, of course, stands alone.) Likewise, in the troll episode, the dwarves first send off their burglar to check things out, and then follow one by one—though as they are captured, they are tied up in sets.

This episode is Bilbo's first venture as a burglar, and he fails miserably by trying to prove his larcenous skills by stealing a purse that turns out to be able to talk. The band is only saved by Gandalf, who illustrates the kind of quick-thinking trickery that Bilbo has just been shown to lack. The whole episode turns out well, however, as the group enriches itself with the trolls' accumulated booty. This first adventure establishes the pattern for the final confrontation with Smaug, the dragon, and also illustrates the qualities that Bilbo will have to acquire in order to fulfill his task.

The band makes its way for rest and recuperation to Rivendell, the Last Homely House, presided over by Elrond the Half-Elven. Here Elrond discovers runic letters, only visible in moonlight, written on Thorin's map. This secret writing reveals that at sunset on Durin's Day, a secret keyhole to the secret door is revealed. The respite in Rivendell establishes another pattern that recurs throughout Tolkien's writing: a period of rest in a safe haven—whether aimed for or fallen upon by accident—after a harrowing experience.

After leaving Rivendell, the band has its first encounter with "goblins"—the beings that later come to be called orcs. In the mountains, caught in a storm, Bilbo and the dwarves take refuge in a cave that appears to be vacant. However, there is a secret door in the back through which the goblins emerge in the dead of night and capture the band. (A bit of business that echoes the goblin attack on Father Christmas's storehouse in 1932.) Gandalf once again saves the dwarves, but in fleeing from the goblins, Bilbo gets lost and encounters a strange being named Gollum and picks up a ring he finds lying in a dark tunnel. Gollum challenges him to a riddle contest, an encounter that truly tests and tempers Bilbo, though he does not realize it at the time.

Tolkien based the riddle contest on good mythological footing: Riddle contests figure in medieval texts as diverse as the German *Der Ring des Nibelungen*, the Norse *Elder Edda* and *King Heidrek's Saga*, and the Old English poem *Solomon and Saturn II*. It is a contest of wits, pure and simple, but Tolkien calls it "sacred," and a man of Tolkien's religious convictions does not use such a word lightly, even in a children's story. A riddle is, at basis, a piece of deliberate ambiguity. In a way, the person who poses the riddle takes something that is whole (for he knows the answer) and unmakes it; his opponent's task is to remake it. However, during the time between the posing of the riddle and its answer, there is a state of chaos, the intellectual equivalent of the time before a Creator gave form to the universe. The answers to Bilbo and Gollum's riddles are mountain, teeth (eating), wind, sun, dark, eggs, fish, time: the substance of existence. Thus, answering a riddle is, in a very small way, taking on a kind of cosmogonic role; likewise, posing a riddle is taking on a somewhat annihilative one. (And the answer to the final question, the one that is not really a riddle, and yet the one that wins the contest for Bilbo, is "the Ring," which turns out ultimately to be of far greater importance for the making and unmaking of the world than anyone realizes.) While the contest continues, the participants trade the powers of creation and destruction back and forth, but when there is a final stumping, one person has both powers for himself.

The contest takes place in the bowels of the earth, not just underground in a safe, hobbity way, but underneath a mountain. This is another pattern repeated over and over in Tolkien's fiction: passing under the earth as a rite of passage. Following a universal cultural pattern, when Bilbo meets Gollum, he undergoes a rite of passage. He is isolated from his companions, in a liminal zone (a place neither Here nor There, on the boundaries, the typical place for rites of passage). He is tested by an elder (for Gollum is both ancient and related to the hobbits) with a threat of death. He acquires a present—the chance-found Ring, Gollum's "Precious." The Ring he acquires will be a useful tool in his new life; it will give him power, but it will also introduce him to moral questions and quests that are far beyond his "childlike" imagination as a simple hobbit. Under the mountain, Bilbo grows up.

No sooner has he obtained the Ring than he is tested once again, the first test of his new life that will set a new pattern. Will he take advantage of his invisibility to kill Gollum? It is the logical thing to do, but it is not the moral thing. Beyond making his decision based on expediency or morality, however, Bilbo decides from compassion, on his "sudden understanding, a pity mixed with horror" of Gollum's life.[6] With that, he makes a leap in the dark that will eventually make him a hero.

The band is reunited, but they are once again attacked by goblins and their allies, the wolf-monsters called wargs. The band is literally treed, and Gandalf's pyrotechnics are turned against them as the goblins pile burning branches at the feet of the trees to smoke the dwarves out. Rescue comes in the form of eagles, summoned by Gandalf, who deposit the party in the vicinity of Beorn's Hall. Beorn is an enigmatic shape-shifter—his name is simply the Anglo-Saxon word for "man" or "warrior" but he can talk to animals and he seems to be able to turn into a bear like the Norse *berserkers* (warriors with "bear shirts" that turn into bears in the frenzy of battle). Gandalf uses the dwarves' trick of showing up in dribs and drabs to trick Beorn into giving the group shelter; once again they have the opportunity to rest and recuperate and are sent on their way with provisions and loaned transport.

At the edge of the Mirkwood, Gandalf leaves the band. With no one but Bilbo to supplement their luck, the dwarves encounter a series of enemies. Lured off the path by elf lights, they are captured by spiders, and only Bilbo's quick thinking—and his magic ring—extricate them. Almost immediately, however, the dwarves are captured by wood-elves, and Bilbo has no notion of what to do but follow invisibly. These episodes illustrate how Bilbo has grown, even though he needs the ring to accomplish his deeds. Rescuing the dwarves from the spiders requires skill in fighting— Bilbo kills the spider that is trying to wrap him up, lures the other spiders with cunning and misdirection until he can free the dwarves, and then kills even more spiders with his sword, Sting. Rescuing the dwarves from the elves requires cunning and planning rather than martial prowess; it needs Gandalf-style trickery. The type of skill required to deal with each adversary also depends on the type of adversary: force against bugs, guile against equals. The threats are also different. The spiders attack the band because they are predators who want to eat them. The imprisonment by the elves, however, is purely the result of a long-standing enmity between elves and dwarves as antagonistic races and is exacerbated by pride and the desire to exhibit power.

After another recuperation and reprovisioning break with the Lake Men of Esgaroth, the dwarves and Bilbo arrive at Lonely Mountain. After the set-up of a secret door, secret letters on the map, and a special day when all will be revealed, all *is* revealed, with the assistance of an inquisitive thrush. Now that the treasure is within reach, it is time for Bilbo to fulfill the task for which he was hired. He goes—alone—to scope out Smaug's hoard and has his first encounter with the dragon.

As an adversary, Smaug incorporates characteristics of both the elves and the spiders. He is "inhuman"—indeed nonmammalian, like the spiders—but his cunning surpasses that of the elves. His greed is for gold, not blood, and his destructiveness is malicious rather than ravenous. While Smaug can cause destruction with his powerful body and his fiery breath, the real danger in him is his subtle mind, capable of turning companions against each other. The enmity between elves and dwarves arises from their differences, their perceptions of each other as enemy races. The danger of the spiders also derives from their difference from the dwarves and the hobbit—so different that the heroes are nothing but food to the spiders. Smaug, in contrast, although alien, is disturbingly similar to his opponents. His lust for gold and treasure is the same emotion felt by dwarves, men, elves, goblins, and wargs. Interestingly, although the "respectable" side of Bilbo is irrevocably bourgeois, the hobbit is the one person who manages to keep his head in the face of all this wealth.

A NEW KIND OF HERO

Bilbo sneaks into the dragon's lair to reconnoiter, and while he is discovered by Smaug and nearly seduced by the dragon's subtle mind games, he also discovers that Smaug has a soft spot on his underbelly where he could be stabbed or shot. Up to this point, Tolkien has followed fairly faithfully a traditional fairy-tale quest plot, albeit a quest tempered with humor and jokes. The end of *The Hobbit* diverges from convention in some interesting ways, however. It seems significant that in his original manuscript, Tolkien wrote almost without break or revision up to the point where Bilbo discovers Smaug's Achilles' heel and then stopped to consider two alternatives for his ending. One was the conclusion of a conventional quest, where Bilbo—as the hero—would be the one who, having discovered the soft spot, slays the dragon. That is what quest heroes do. In the other version, the one that Tolkien chose, Smaug is killed by the Lake Man Bard, the descendant of the King of the Dales, who is told of the soft spot by the same thrush who revealed the keyhole to the Lonely Mountain and stayed around to do a little eavesdropping. At this point, Tolkien put the manuscript aside and did not write any further for quite some time. He apparently came up with an oral ending for the story that he told to the children, but it is as though, having "broken with tradition" in the dragon's death, he was not sure where to go, or not sure that he wanted to go there. In 1932, he showed the manuscript to a few people, including Lewis (who was characteristically enthusiastic) and a former student named Elaine Griffiths. In 1936, probably around four years after Tolkien abandoned the Hobbit manuscript, Griffiths happened to mention to Susan Dagnall, a college friend now working for the publishing house of Allen & Unwin, that Professor Tolkien had written a wonderful children's story that really should be published. Dagnall persuaded Tolkien to lend her the manuscript and found that she agreed on its merits. She sent it back to Tolkien, urging him to finish the story so that it could be published, preferably within the year. For Tolkien, the prospect of publishing a book that might help alleviate some of his chronic money worries was enough to overcome his habitual procrastination in composition, and by the beginning of October the completed manuscript was in Allen & Unwin's hands. Tolkien had chosen an interesting way of winding up his tale.

The slaying of the dragon should have been the culmination of the quest, after which the hero gets his reward and "happily ever after" looms on the horizon. Instead, Smaug's death merely attracts a horde of armies anxious to pick over the loot, more like the greedy relatives who descend upon the death of a wealthy man in some Victorian novel than the protagonists of a heroic legend.

Given that Tolkien had followed the conventions of the quest tale so faithfully up to this point—granted, with humor and a certain irony in his choice of hero—and given that, with his background, he certainly knew the conventions inside and out, it must be assumed that he took this unexpected turn into left field for a reason. After Bilbo discovers the soft spot in Smaug, his real function is to resolve the high emotions and impasse that the release of all that treasure arouses. He does it with trickery, pocketing the Arkenstone—the primary dwarvish treasure—by luck and using it to engineer a truce, and he carries out his negotiations in his most businesslike hobbit manner. Although he does not act like an epic, or even a folktale hero, he gets the job done. In so doing, not only does Bilbo make it possible for the squabbling forces of good—the dwarf, elf, and human armies—to join forces against the real evil forces of goblins and wargs, but he also, in a way, engineers the redemption of the dwarves from their gold lust, the taint that has infected them from the dragon treasure.

In subverting the conventional pattern of the quest tale and confounding the reader's expectations of heroism, Tolkien firmly draws attention to the value of the mundane, nonheroic qualities that Bilbo embodies. As noted before, for all his conventional and bourgeois ethics, Bilbo is remarkable in his lack of interest in money and his lack of desire for power. His idea of a happy life is a very moderate middle course between austerity and luxury. Although he has undergone a rite of passage and become a hero, he has retained a clear sense of practicality and common sense. These, Tolkien seems to be saying, are the real attributes of a hero.

Yet, although Bilbo may not slay the real dragon, he does have his chance to rout the dragon-greedy in his own home when he finally returns to Bag End and discovers his possessions up for auction and the Sackville-Bagginses about to take possession of his highly desirable hobbit hole. All the dangers out there in the macrocosm of the wider world are lurking, microcosmically, at home.

Although Tolkien did not realize it when he first wrote of the encounter between Bilbo and Gollum in the depths of the mountain, this seemingly minor plot twist held the key to the entire edifice that later became *The Lord of the Rings*. Just as Smaug is, in many ways, a monstrous extreme of the dwarves' desire for gold, so Gollum is, from the very beginning, a monstrous distortion of a hobbit. Indeed, he later turns out to be a kind of ancestral hobbit, an Ur-hobbit. Normal hobbits live in holes, burrows, or warrens in the ground; Gollum lives in the deepest, darkest hole of all. Yet normal hobbits (except for the Brandybucks family) are leery of the water, and Gollum is a water creature, so he is disturbingly the same as a hobbit, yet disturbingly different as well.

Bilbo's encounter with Gollum prepares him for his encounter with Smaug, which is, after all, the real purpose of the journey. Bilbo has been hired as a burglar to go down inside a mountain, match wits with a monster, and recover a treasure. This is exactly what happens when he inadvertently meets Gollum. The difference is that the dwarves have hired him to take care of a monster whose monstrosity is a corruption of their own natures, not of Bilbo's, and thus, in a way, they are attempting to circumvent or deny the possibility of corruption and monstrosity in themselves; naturally (by fairy-tale logic), this means that they fall prey to it instantly when they see the treasure hoard. The gold-lust aroused in them, especially in Thorin, makes them refuse to even consider any kind of compensation for the Lake Men, who have suffered from the effects of the dwarves' quest and who, as the descendants of the Dale Men, are entitled to the recovery of their dragon-stolen treasure as much as the dwarves are. Tolkien's "fairy tale" turns out to have the same underpinning of myth that he and Lewis had aimed for in their science fiction enterprise.

MAKING BOOK

The chairman of Allen & Unwin, Stanley Unwin, believed in getting review opinions of manuscripts from the audience to whom he intended to sell the books, and so he offered his ten-year-old son Rayner a shilling to review *The Hobbit: Or, There and Back Again.* In his opinion, "This book, with the help of maps, does not need any illustration it is good and should appeal to all children between the ages of 5 and 9."[7] The manuscript was accepted. (It was, however, decided that illustrations might, after all, be a nice addition, and Tolkien provided them.)

The publication process of *The Hobbit* was an eye-opener for both Tolkien and Allen & Unwin. Tolkien was remarkably naive about the economics of commercial publishing and was constantly surprised and disappointed at being told that his pictures were too expensive to reproduce or that his preferred method of placement for the maps could not be accommodated. He also had an unfortunate habit, which could have been predicted by anyone who knew him, of making extensive revisions in proof—an extremely expensive habit that required resetting the type for all the pages with changes. Tolkien was extremely careful to make his rewrites take up exactly the same amount of space on the page as the eliminated text, in hopes of easing the typesetters' work, but in the days when letters made of metal slugs were literally set by hand into a form to create the words that were printed on a page, any rewrite in the proof stage involved an enormous amount of work.

The Hobbit was published on September 17, 1937. Tolkien was worried about his colleagues' reaction to his publication of a children's book rather than the monograph on some aspect of Anglo-Saxon philology that most professors in his position would be expected to produce. However, his colleagues appeared to be completely oblivious of the fact that he had published anything, much less something outside of his field.

The one denizen of Oxford who noticed the book was, of course, C. S. Lewis, who took advantage of his position as a regular reviewer for the *Times Literary Supplement* to write reviews for both the *TLS* and the *Times*. The book was almost universally well reviewed (there were naturally a few dissenters), and by Christmas it was sold out and on to its second printing. An American edition came out early in 1938, published by Houghton Mifflin, and was equally successful. Within months, it was realized that *The Hobbit* was a best-seller. And where best-sellers tread, sequels must follow.

NOTES

1. Carpenter, *Biography*, 162.

2. J.R.R. Tolkien, *The Father Christmas Letters*, edited by Baillie Tolkien (Boston: Houghton Mifflin, 1976), np.

3. Carpenter, *Letters*, 377.

4. Carpenter, *Letters*, 172.

5. J.R.R. Tolkien, *The Lost Road and Other Writings*, edited by Christopher Tolkien (Boston: Houghton Mifflin, 1987), 39–116.

6. J.R.R. Tolkien, *The Hobbit* (London: G. Allen & Unwin, 1937), 80.

7. Carpenter, *Biography*, 184.

Chapter 8

THE WAR OF THE RINGS
(1937–1955)

Stanley Unwin was eager to follow the success of *The Hobbit* and was happy to discover that Tolkien had several manuscripts in various stages of completion that might be suitable. Tolkien sent him "The Silmarillion," "Mr. Bliss," "Roverandom," the few chapters he had written of "The Lost Road," and a story called "Farmer Giles of Ham." While the children's stories were deemed publishable, none of them was about hobbits, and Unwin was convinced that what the public wanted was more hobbits.

As for The Silmarillion, the reader who reviewed that manuscript was nonplused. The "Celtic" names of the characters were off-putting, and the sections written in verse were embarrassingly old-fashioned in his opinion. On the other hand, where an actual plot could be discerned, the tale was gripping. It was also unmistakably set in the same fictional universe as *The Hobbit,* even though there were (as yet) no hobbits in it. Unwin suggested to Tolkien that "it is a mine to be explored in writing further books like *The Hobbit* rather than a book in itself."[1]

Tolkien was intrigued by the idea of more hobbits in Middle-earth, although as far as he was concerned there was a problem of tone: Hobbits were comic, The Silmarillion was serious. Yet he started writing almost immediately a first draft of a story about Bilbo called "A Long Expected Party." However, he really did not have much of a plot in mind yet. Bilbo was to use his ring of invisibility to slip away from his birthday party in order to go replenish his store of dragon-gold. As he wrote, he began to realize that Bilbo's transformation into a hero in the previous book did not leave very much room for further evolution; perhaps it would be better to have this new adventure focus on the next generation, Bilbo's son or nephew. Since his original plan had involved the use of the ring, perhaps the ring was the key to this new adventure. After all, where had it come from? Wasn't it a rather peculiar item for Gollum, lurking under his mountain, to have obtained? Although its invisibility-conferring powers were useful (and highly traditional), might it not have other properties of a more sinister bent? Invisibility is power and power corrupts; there had already been hints that Gandalf was involved in some off-stage maneuvering against Sauron the "Necromancer"; could he be the ultimate source of the ring? By February 1938, he had a first chapter featuring Bilbo's nephew Bingo Bolger-Baggins (a name that sounds more like one devised by P. G. Wodehouse—the creator of such characters as Catsmeat Potter Purbright, Gussie Fink-Nottle, and Tuppy Glossop, not to mention Bingo Little—than by Tolkien). He sent the story draft off to Unwin, who passed it to his son Rayner, the original reviewer of *The Hobbit*. The story met with Rayner's approval, and Unwin gave Tolkien the go-ahead.

THE "NEW HOBBIT"

The early part of 1938 saw work on the "New Hobbit" proceeding at what, for Tolkien, was a fairly swift pace. He was forced to do his writing late at night, when everyone else had gone to bed and his academic duties were concluded for the day. There were distractions in his private life as well. Christopher was diagnosed with a heart condition that required him to return home from boarding school, and Tolkien, always an involved father, spent a great deal of time caring for his son. His friend and old collaborator Eric Gordon died unexpectedly late in the year, and Tolkien took over the task of setting and grading the Honours Examinations for the students he had left behind. He was uncomfortably aware of his lifelong tendency to start off writing projects that seemed promising at first but ultimately went nowhere. There were several incentives to keep going and complete the sequel that countered the distractions, however. With four children in various stages of education—and he sent them all to Catholic boarding schools—an Oxford don's salary did not go far, and any income from novel writing would be more than welcome (and much less tedious to earn than marking School Certificates). The Inklings were in what might be called their heyday, and the support and feedback he received from reading his manuscripts in their meetings helped to keep his momentum going. But there was also an element of competition in the Inklings, especially with Lewis.

Lewis was a very fast writer; during the time that Tolkien was writing *The Hobbit*, Lewis had produced two books of literary criticism (*The Pil-*

grim's Regress in 1933 and The Allegory of Love in 1936) and completed his space-travel novel, while Tolkien's time-travel effort had gone nowhere. Tolkien had recommended Lewis's novel to his own publisher, and while Allen & Unwin rejected it, Stanley Unwin had passed it on to another publishing house with which he was connected, Bodley Head, and Out of the Silent Planet was published in 1938. As Tolkien struggled in the twelve-year morass that became the writing of The Lord of the Rings, Lewis published two more science fiction novels, the seven Narnia books, The Screwtape Letters, and fourteen works of nonfiction, many of them religious works. Tolkien's pleasure at his friend's return to Christianity was fading as the irreconcilable differences in their respective faiths became ever more evident. Lewis's growing friendship with Charles Williams also drove a wedge between the two. Tolkien was not as enthusiastic about the quality of Williams's fiction as Lewis was, and he was put off by Williams's admittedly weird take on Christianity. Lewis was a man who made friends fast and easily, but aside from his brother, Warnie, and his childhood friend Arthur Greeves, his friendships had a tendency to burn out after an initial period of intensity. Tolkien, in contrast, made his friends (as opposed to his rapid accumulation of allies among his colleagues) slowly and expected them to last. He appears to have felt that Lewis abandoned, or at least downgraded, their friendship in his enthusiasm for Williams.

Complicating the relationship between the two friends was Edith. She and Lewis had never liked each other for reasons that were never entirely clear. It may well have been that Lewis epitomized everything that Edith found intimidating and off-putting about the highly intellectualized society of Oxford; Edith, from Lewis's point of view, may well have seemed completely inconsequential with her life completely devoted to her family. (There is no record of what the Tolkiens, for their part, thought of Lewis's relationship with Mrs. Moore.)

Furthermore, Edith had been growing increasingly dissatisfied with the tenor of her life in Oxford. Devotion to hearth and home had not been her only goal in life. As a young woman she had intended to be a professional pianist; the years she spent on her own before her marriage had given her a taste of independence that had disappeared as she settled into the role of wife and mother. She had converted to Catholicism out of devotion to Tolkien, not out of any religious conviction, and over the years her tolerance for the religion had faded as Tolkien's own piety had increased. As her own shyness prevented her from forming close friendships in Oxford, her resentment of Tolkien's male friendships increased, especially her antipathy towards his closest friend, Lewis. In 1940, the Tolkiens blew up in a major row; Edith finally expressed her feelings about her life and her dislike of Catholicism; the fight ended in a reconciliation and an agreement that Edith would follow her own religious leanings (she ceased attending Catholic services, but did not return to the Anglican church); it may well be that his renewed understanding of his wife's jealousy of his male friendships also contributed to Tolkien's disillusion with Lewis.

By the end of the summer of 1938, Tolkien had brought the events in his new story as far as the inn at Bree, where his hobbits—he was now considering whether to change Bingo's name to Frodo—encountered an enigmatic character named Trotter. He was still not certain why Bilbo's ring was so important, however, and since the ring seemed to be driving the plot of the story, this was a rather important piece of motivation. Suddenly it struck him: This was the lost One Ring that ruled all the other rings, Sauron's own Ring, and in order to neutralize Sauron's evil power, the Ring must be taken back to Mordor, the vile wasteland ruled by Sauron, and destroyed in the volcanic fires where it was forged. Now he knew where he was going, and now he knew the name of his story: The Lord of the Rings. The stakes were higher than in *The Hobbit*, and thus the tone was darker, he warned his publisher.

WAR AND AFTER

World War II disrupted much more than writing schedules throughout Britain. Oxford was lucky that Hitler decided not to bomb the university town, but rationing affected everyone, and evacuees from the Blitz required housing in every available room. The oldest of the Tolkiens' sons, John, was studying for the priesthood in Rome when war erupted; he and his fellow students were evacuated to Lancashire. The two younger boys were still of college age when war broke out, but when they were old enough, Michael became an anti-aircraft gunner and Christopher joined the air force. Their rooms in the house at Northmoor Road were often occupied by evacuees and lodgers. Tolkien's prime writing time, the small hours of the night, were preempted by air warden duty. Although the university did not shudder to a standstill as it had during World War I, academic life changed radically as service cadets, who needed academic credentials in order to become officers, were sent to Oxford for "short courses" to give them their qualifications.

Tolkien continued writing when he could, but by late 1940 he had reached a standstill, around the point where the Fellowship—Frodo and his eight companions—reaches Balin's tomb in Moria. It was the first of several hiatuses in his writing. When he resumed writing after almost a year, he tried outlining the rest of the story as he then saw it and anticipated that he was only a few chapters from the end. Yet by the summer of 1943, he was still writing, and he was stuck again. Writing resumed in April 1944, and when Christopher was sent to South Africa for training that summer, his father sent him sections of manuscript and letters describing his progress. By the time the narrative reached Shelob's lair, Tolkien was tapped out. There was little writing accomplished in 1945. The end of the war brought joy, but the day after the European war came to an end, Charles Williams was taken ill. He died six days later, on May 15. Although the two had not been close, they had been companions, and Tolkien felt his loss.

Another notable occurrence of 1945 was Tolkien's appointment as Merton Professor of English Language and Literature. This shifted his locus of operations from Pembroke, where he had never felt particularly comfortable, to Merton College, which was much more informal. Later that year the Merton Professorship of English Literature fell vacant, and it was widely felt that Lewis was one of the prime candidates for the position, but he was passed over. The schism between Tolkien and Lewis started to become noticeable at this point. After Lewis was elected to the chair of Medieval and Renaissance Literature at Cambridge in 1954 (a position that was essentially created for him, partly in recompense for the loss of the Merton chair), the two rarely saw each other, although Lewis was an enthusiastic reviewer of *The Lord of the Rings* when it was finally published.

Another benefit of Tolkien's new professorship was that Merton College had houses available to rent to its fellows, and since the house in Northmoor Road was now far too large and expensive to maintain with only Christopher and Priscilla living at home, the Tolkiens put in an application for a Merton house. In 1947, they were able to move into a smaller house, in Manor Road near the center of town, but it soon became clear that the house was *too* small. Housing was very tight in Britain in the postwar years, and although they put in another application for a better house when one should come available, for the time being, they just had to make do. One of the primary drawbacks of the new house was the lack of a suitable study for Tolkien.

Another postwar development was Rayner Unwin's arrival in Oxford as an undergraduate. He had made Tolkien's acquaintance, and since he had been his earliest and most enthusiastic reviewer, Tolkien gave him the manuscript of The Lord of the Rings as far as it went. Rayner's enthusiasm was undimmed with age, and he assured his father that the final story—which Allen & Unwin had more or less despaired of ever receiving—would be worth the wait. Tolkien decided to try to finish the manuscript, but first, he decided that he needed to revise what he already had. He also decided to revise *The Hobbit* to make the Gollum episode conform to the plot as it had subsequently evolved. However, by the autumn of 1949, nearly a dozen years since the Hobbit sequel had first been proposed, the manuscript was finished, typed up, and ready to go to the publisher.

PUBLISHING FOLLIES

There was a question in Tolkien's mind, however, as to which publisher it should go to. Despite his established relationship with Allen & Unwin, he was, like so many authors throughout time, dissatisfied with his publisher's support of his brainchildren. Allen & Unwin's lack of interest in The Silmarillion rankled, increasingly so as Tolkien realized that the close interrelationship of The Silmarillion and The Lord of the Rings made the publication of the former desirable as backstory for the latter. At the end of the war, Allen & Unwin had agreed to bring out Tolkien's story Farmer Giles of Ham, which ultimately was published in 1949, but Tolkien was dissatisfied with the firm's lack of publicity for it and also with the quality of the first postwar edition of *The Hobbit*, which lacked the illustrations of the original. Part of the problem was not Allen & Unwin's fault: paper was in short supply not only during the war but for many years afterward, and it was not economically feasible to publish on the scale that had been possible before the war. Tolkien, however, had very little understanding of the realities of publishing economics, and Allen & Unwin had very little understanding of Tolkien's emotional investment in Middle-earth.

Late in 1949, Tolkien sent the manuscript of The Silmarillion to Milton Wadman of Collins Publishers. Wadman, who was Catholic, had been introduced to Tolkien by a sometime Inkling, Gervase Mathew, who was a Dominican priest. Wadman was interested to hear of Tolkien's proposed sequel to the successful *Hobbit*, although he probably had not expected to be handed The Silmarillion first. Once he had expressed interest in the first manuscript, however, Tolkien sent him the second, and Wadman liked that one even better. Furthermore, Collins had an edge over Allen & Unwin in that, as stationers as well as publishers, they had a larger paper ration than most publishers. Given the enormous length of the two manuscripts, this was no small consideration.

Once Collins had expressed interest in publishing the books, Tolkien had to come up with a way to disengage himself from Allen & Unwin. In 1950, he began writing a series of discouraging letters to his erstwhile publishers, announcing he had decided that The Lord of the Rings and The Silmarillion must be published together, and that despite the excessive length of the total work (which he estimated at one million words, about the size of a three-volume encyclopedia), they must be published whole— the only possible division would be into two volumes; the two works could not be subdivided. He also suggested that no one outside of his immediate circle of friends would be particularly interested in reading such a long and complex work. Certainly the manuscripts he had now produced were hardly what had been meant by a "sequel" to The Hobbit—and in this he was not exaggerating. Allen & Unwin had already rejected Roverandom and Mr. Bliss, undeniably children's books, as not Hobbit-y enough; The Lord of the Rings, despite the presence of hobbits, was light-years away in tone and style, The Silmarillion in another solar system altogether. Finally, in April 1950, stung by a suggestion from Rayner Unwin that the publishing house buy both manuscripts and then drop The Silmarillion after a second look (and why Stanley Unwin passed this suggestion on to Tolkien boggles the imagination; tantamount to announcing in advance that they planned to take advantage of him), Tolkien demanded a firm yes or no on his nonnegotiable terms. Unwin said no.

Tolkien was now free to offer his manuscripts officially to Collins. However, now that the fish was hooked, Collins announced that The Lord of the Rings required cutting. Tolkien, dismayed, agreed to give it his best shot, but countered by sending along several more chapters of The Silmarillion. With author and editor already lurching towards cross-purposes, Wadman left for Italy, where he lived for most of the year. Then Wadman became ill and was not able to make his annual autumn trip to London. Publication of the completed manuscript was going nowhere, while Tolkien was still working on completing The Silmarillion (growing ever longer). Unwin, hearing that things were not going smoothly over at Collins, made overtures to Tolkien again, but Tolkien was not ready to give up on his new publishers. However, by March 1952, he still had not signed a contract with Collins, and the price of paper was rising, making the publication of long books increasingly unprofitable. Finally, Tolkien once again issued an ultimatum, demanding that Collins publish The Lord of the Rings immediately or he would return to Allen & Unwin. William Collins, the owner of the company, who had begun to gauge Tolkien's difficulty as an author, regretfully told him that perhaps returning to Allen & Unwin would be best for him.

THERE AND BACK AGAIN

Now, of course, Tolkien had to mend the fences he had gone to such lengths to break. Fortunately, Rayner Unwin, graduated and working for the family firm, was open to his overtures. In fact, once he got his hands on the manuscript, he did not even bother rereading it, but set straight to work estimating production costs. He came to the conclusion that the best way—the most economical way—to publish the book would be to divide it into three separate volumes, each selling for the high price of twenty-one shillings each. This allowed Allen & Unwin a small profit margin, assuming that the book sold out its print run; if it did not sell, the publisher stood to lose up to a thousand pounds. However, Rayner argued to his father that *The Lord of the Rings* would bring the company a good deal of prestige, which was also a consideration. The company decided to publish the entire manuscript—no cuts, as Collins had requested—in three volumes, and offered Tolkien a profit-sharing contract. Rather than conventional royalties, which are calculated as a percentage of the cover price of all volumes sold, Tolkien would receive no payments until the costs of production had been recouped; after that, he would receive 50 percent of all profits. If the volumes sold poorly, as Allen & Unwin feared, their losses would be minimized, but if they sold well, Tolkien stood to make far more money than he would with a conventional contract.

The publication process now began. The Tolkiens were in the middle of their third move in five years; after leaving the too-small house in Manor Road for a larger house around the corner in Holywell Street in 1950, the traffic noise in the new house turned out to be unbearable. (Tolkien likened it to living in Mordor.) In March 1953, the Tolkiens moved to Headington, the same eastern Oxford suburb where Lewis's house, The Kilns, was located. Nonetheless, Tolkien managed to make the revisions that were needed for the first two volumes, *The Fellowship of the Ring* and *The Two Towers*, by the end of spring. Then he had to cope with the proofs—the typesetters had once again "corrected" his spellings of words such as "dwarves" and "elvish" to "dwarfs" and "elfish," and so on. There were also problems with both planned and unplanned illustrations. Tolkien had hoped to include such fine touches as red letters for the fiery letters on the Ring and the presentation of the dwarvish chronicle found in Moria as a facsimile, carefully prepared by Tolkien in a variety of "manuscript hands" and alphabets, complete with artistically burned page edges and splatters of "blood" where the chronicle came to its tragic conclusion. These proved to be too expensive for an already high-priced publication; it was agreed that maps would be a useful addition, but Tolkien found it difficult to complete these, and the job was eventually turned over to Christopher Tolkien.

Allen & Unwin planned to bring out *The Fellowship of the Ring* in the summer of 1954, to be followed by the other two volumes at short intervals. The first two volumes were all ready to print, but the final volume, *The Return of the King*, was advertised as containing appendixes that were yet to be written. The publication of *The Fellowship of the Ring* in early August, 1954, was followed with generally positive reviews. Most reviewers, even those who were dismissive of Tolkien's prose style, admitted that the plot was enough to carry the book and looked forward to the second installment. Within six weeks of publication, it was necessary to order another print run, as the original run of 3,500 copies had sold out. Meanwhile, Tolkien was traveling over the summer—he received honorary degrees from the National University of Ireland and the University of Lièges—and was unable to proceed with his appendixes. *The Two Towers* came out in November and received the same type of reviews as the first volume, and those who had read both were now on tenterhooks waiting for the rest of the story: The second book ended with Frodo captured by orcs and Sam trapped with the Ring in Shelob's lair. By March, when *The Return of the King* had not appeared, Allen & Unwin was receiving letters of complaint from readers who wanted to know when the suspense would be relieved, and Tolkien was still working on the appendixes. He finally delivered them on March 20, 1955, and then took Edith and Priscilla on a holiday to Italy, where the proofs and printer's queries followed him from pillar to post; even when they caught up with him, he was unable to deal with them until he reached home and was reunited with his notes. *The Return of the King* was published on October 20 (minus the promised index), making a full critical assessment of the trilogy possible. Houghton Mifflin had been the American publisher, as with *The Hobbit*, and critique from the other side of the Atlantic also poured in.

LOVE AND HATE

From the very beginning, opinion was divided on the trilogy's artistic merit. C. S. Lewis and W. H. Auden both loved it; aside from their personal connection to Tolkien (Auden had taken his lectures as an Oxford undergraduate and experimented in Old English alliteration in some of his early poems under the influence of Tolkien's impressive classroom readings of *Beowulf*), both men were very fond of genre fiction such as science fiction and murder mysteries. Edwin Muir, the reviewer in the British *Observer*, and Edmund Wilson, in the American *Nation*, disliked the books intensely, regarding them as Boys' Own Stories (that is, naïve, adventurous moral tales) written in quasi-biblical prose. For reviewers such as these, *The Lord of the Rings* was a return to the naively heroic stance of pre–World War I fantasy, such as Tolkien's inspirations, William Morris, Lord Dunsany, and E.R. Eddison, or H. Rider Haggard's colonialist adventures such as *She* and *King Solomon's Mines*. Part of the problem was that Tolkien actually was, in a sense, trying to write in that now-outdated genre, and part of the problem was that those who were committed to the agenda of modernist literature were never going to be impressed by a medievalist epic. Another problem, one which took some time to sink in for Tolkien, was that Lewis's gushing reviews—proclaiming the books "like lightning from a clear sky ... gorgeous, eloquent, and unashamed"[2] and "too original and too opulent for any final judgement on first reading"[3]— had antagonized reviewers who had no bone to pick with Tolkien but roundly detested Lewis. Anything Lewis liked was therefore automatically beneath contempt.

The dichotomy between Tolkien-lovers and Tolkien-despisers, which to a large extent broke with readers on the first side and professional critics and academics on the other, continued long after Tolkien's death. The election of *The Lord of the Rings* as "the book of the century" and Tolkien as "the most influential author of the twentieth century" in polls taken in Britain in the late 1990s aroused such responses as "Oh hell," and "my nightmare" (the latter from feminist literary critic and commentator Germaine Greer) among the literati.[4] Even those who appreciate the books tend to focus on the completeness of Tolkien's subcreation, the way the reader becomes absorbed into Middle-earth as a real place with languages and legends. In many ways, both camps tend to overlook the enormous skill that underlies Tolkien's creations, the careful patterning of themes and characters to present a work of art crafted as elaborately as the Middle English poems *Pearl* and *Cleanness*, which were as much his inspiration as *Beowulf* or the Eddas.

NOTES

1. Carpenter, *Biography*, 188.

2. C.S. Lewis, "The Gods Return to Earth," *Time & Tide* 35 (August 14, 1954): 1082–83.

3. C.S. Lewis, "The Dethronement of Power," *Time & Tide* 36 (October 22, 1956): 1373–74.

4. T.A. Shippey, *J.R.R. Tolkien: Author of the Century* (Boston: Houghton Mifflin, 2001), xx–xxiv.

Chapter 9

THE QUEST TO OVERTHROW EVIL

Like *The Hobbit*, *The Lord of the Rings* is a quest story. Bilbo's quest (wished on him by Gandalf and the dwarves) is to get to the Lonely Mountain and steal treasure away; Frodo's quest (wished on him—though freely accepted—by Gandalf and the Council of Elrond) is to get to Mount Doom and destroy a treasure. Neither hobbit really understands what he has gotten himself into when he begins the quest; both are irreversibly altered by their journeys.

Despite the increasing complexity of the narrative structure as the story progresses, the overall plot is fairly simple. After Bilbo leaves the Shire, bequeathing his home and his ring to his nephew Frodo, Gandalf discovers that the ring is not just any ring, but the One Ring that holds the key to the power held by the necromancer Sauron. In order to prevent this arch-evil from prevailing, the Ring must be destroyed, and that can only be accomplished by casting it back into the volcanic fires of Mount Doom in Mordor, where the Ring was forged. Gandalf and Frodo decide that the Ring must be taken to Rivendell, where Elrond Half-Elven, the son of Eärendil, may advise them on how this larger quest can best be accomplished.

Frodo attempts to leave the Shire surreptitiously, but his plans are overthrown by two occurrences, one threatening and one helpful. Mysterious "Black Riders" appear in the Shire, and they are seeking "Bagginssss"; their intentions are patently malevolent. Frodo's friends and cousins, Meriadoc "Merry" Brandybuck and Peregrine "Pippin" Took, and his servant, Samwise Gamgee, discover his plans to strike out alone and conspire to accompany him. With the Black Riders on their tail, the company leaves the Shire and promptly gets lost in the Old Forest, where they are nearly consumed by Old Man Willow and saved by Tom Bombadil. On the way from Tom's house to Bree, where they hope to meet up with Gandalf, they are captured again, this time by the Barrow Wight, and again rescued by Tom. In Bree, Gandalf is nowhere to be found, and Frodo is lured by the Ring into revealing himself. Fortunately, while this calls the attention of the Black Riders' confederates, it also brings them the assistance of the Ranger named Strider. He undertakes to chaperone them to Rivendell, a place that is not reached without some harrowing harrying by the Black Riders. Frodo is wounded by their swords, a wound that will trouble him for the rest of his life.

At Rivendell, Frodo is healed, and the party is reunited with Bilbo and Gandalf. Strider is revealed as Aragorn, the unthroned king of Minas Tirith. Representatives of other races have also arrived, troubled by their own perceptions of rising evil: The elves have lost Gollum, entrusted to them for imprisonment; the dwarves are concerned that Balin, who set off to refound the dwarvish city of Moria, has not been heard from; and the men of Minas Tirith are overwhelmed by their attempts to ward off the predations of Sauron. When the Council of Elrond is assembled and the discovery of the Ring is discussed, it is decided that a Fellowship will be formed to accompany the Ringbearer—Frodo—at least part way to Mount Doom; at some point, Boromir of Minas Tirith and Aragorn will split off to address the related problem of war with Sauron. The Fellowship consists of two men (Aragorn and Boromir), a wizard (Gandalf), an elf (Legolas), a dwarf (Gimli, son of Bilbo's old companion Glóin), and the four hobbits (Frodo, Sam, Merry, and Pippin).

The Fellowship is forced to route their journey through Moria, where it is discovered that Balin's colony has been wiped out by orcs, and where Gandalf is lost in a battle with a Balrog. The company makes its way to Lothlórien, where they are individually "tested" and given gifts by the elf queen Galadriel. After this break for rest and recuperation, the fellowship moves on, but it is clear that Boromir is becoming obsessed with possessing the Ring. His attempt to take it from Frodo causes the hobbit to decide that the only safe way to accomplish his mission is to carry on alone; Sam, however, will not let his master abandon him. An orc ambush scatters the rest of the Fellowship: Boromir redeems himself in death by defending Merry and Pippin, although the two hobbits are nonetheless captured; Aragorn, Gimli, and Legolas decide to honor Frodo's decision to carry on alone and follow the orcs to rescue Merry and Pippin.

These two hobbits, meanwhile, manage to escape their captors when the orcs are ambushed by the men of Rohan; taking refuge in the Forest of

Fangorn, they encounter the Ent Treebeard. The stories the hobbits tell of the wizard Saruman's corruption, uncovered by Gandalf, provides the catalyst for the Ents to take action themselves. Aragorn, Gimli, and Legolas, meanwhile, encounter Gandalf, mystically reborn from his fall in Moria. This group makes its way to Rohan, where Gandalf masterminds the recovery of its king, Théoden, fallen into decrepitude under the influence of Saruman's agent, Gríma Wormtongue. Here, too, Théoden's niece Éowyn first sees and falls unrequitedly in love with Aragorn.

The men of Rohan take off to quell Saruman, but after battling orcs at the Battle of Helm's Deep, on arrival at Isengard they find the place destroyed by Ents. Gandalf, Aragorn, Legolas, Gimli, Merry, and Pippin are reunited. Saruman attempts to talk his way out of the consequences of his betrayal, but his spell is broken. The group breaks up again, with the forces of Rohan, accompanied by Merry, returning home to muster for the upcoming war against Sauron. Aragorn, Gandalf, and Pippin head for Minas Tirith.

Meanwhile, Frodo and Sam are making their way to Mordor, tailed, as they come to realize, by Gollum. Frodo captures Gollum and uses the power of the Ring to extract his promise to guide them to Mordor, but when they arrive at the front way in, so to speak, there is no way to enter. Caught in the backwash of a battle between Sauron's forces and an army from Minas Tirith, the hobbits are captured by Boromir's much wiser brother Faramir. Faced with the same temptation to take the Ring that proved his brother's downfall, Faramir passes the test and sends the hobbits on their way with supplies. Gollum takes them to the pass of Cirith Ungol, where he betrays them to Shelob, the mother of all monster spiders. Believing Frodo dead, Sam takes the Ring (an act that he justifies as carrying on his master's quest, but which has overtones of Ringly manipulation in order to gain itself a Bearer); too late, he discovers that Frodo is not dead, only paralyzed by Shelob's sting, and Sam is left locked out of Mordor. This is the point where the story stopped while Tolkien tried to complete the appendixes and index for the final volume, an unintentional cliff-hanger.

MODERN INTERLACE

The story begins by following the adventures of one character, Frodo, and those who accompany him. As the story progresses and the Fellowship fragments, so does the narrative point of view. One interesting consistency, however, is that Tolkien invariably narrates his scenes from the "lowest" point of view available—often literally, from the point of view of the shortest character present, whether hobbit or dwarf, or of the youngest. As Frodo becomes increasingly matured and wearied by his role as Ringbearer, the point of view in these scenes shifts from Frodo to the much more naive Sam. Whether this was an intentional authorial strategy or not, it serves to make Tolkien's potentially stultifying tale of the power politics in an imaginary realm personal and immediate. The reader knows no more about the struggle between Mordor and Gondor than do the hobbits, isolated as they are in the Shire, and so the events are presented from a point of view consonant with the reader's perspective without an overreliance on plot-killing exposition.

The first subsection (or "book") of *The Return of the King* takes the dispersed yet interrelated plot strands to their limits. In many ways, the plot here recalls the medieval technique of interlace, with which Tolkien was intimately familiar from his work on *Sir Gawain, Pearl,* and *Cleanness.* Gandalf and Pippin travel to Minas Tirith, ruled by the steward Denethor, the father of Boromir and Faramir. Pippin offers his fealty to Denethor, stung by the nobleman's apparent disdain for his small stature. Pippin now must learn the life of a soldier in a standing army—as opposed to the life of a warrior, such as Aragorn, which is all he has ever seen. An unnatural darkness spreads over the city.

Meanwhile, Merry also swears fealty—to Théoden. While Pippin is inspired from a desire to prove that his valor outweighs his stature, Merry's oath arises out of pure love for a man who has transcended his infirmities and is making a final stand for his principles.

At the same time, several Rangers intercept Théoden's army and deliver a message to Aragorn from Elrond: "If thou art in haste, remember the Paths of the Dead."[1] These Dead are the spirits of men who had foresworn their allegiance to Isildur in the first war against Sauron; summoning them will allow them to finally fulfill their oath and let them rest in peace. After revealing himself to Sauron as the Returned King by looking into the *palantír* of Orthanc, Aragorn precedes the army to Edoras, where Éowyn attempts, unsuccessfully, to dissuade him from his path. Her failure reinforces Éowyn's feelings of abandonment and despair.

Simultaneously, Théoden and his army prepare to set out from Dunharrow, where Éowyn has taken the civilians of Rohan for safety, to the aid of Minas Tirith. Despite Merry's oath to him, Théoden will not take Merry into battle, however. A mysterious young warrior called Dernhelm offers to sneak Merry along with him.

For his part, Pippin attends upon his new lord, Denethor. He and his friend Beregond see Faramir attacked by five Black Riders and rescued by Gandalf. Faramir reports his encounter with Frodo and Sam; Gandalf is troubled, but Denethor is enraged. Boromir's confidence that he alone could withstand the evil influence of the Ring was evidently an inherited trait. The Siege of Gondor begins: Cair Andros falls, as do the city's outer defenses. Faramir is wounded not only by weapons but by the Black Breath of the Nazgûl. Denethor goes mad, decides that all is lost, and commands his men to take Faramir—ill but alive—to the mausoleum of the kings and stewards of Gondor, where he intends to burn the two of them alive on a funeral pyre. Pippin finds Gandalf in the act of defying the Lord of the Nazgûl to enter the city. And the horns of Rohan are heard with the first cockcrow of the unexpected dawn.

Meanwhile, the army of Rohan has been led to Gondor by the Wild Men, and their arrival instigates the Battle of the Pelennor Fields. The Lord of the Nazgûl is diverted from breaking the gate of Gondor to face this new assault. Théoden's horse, terrorized by the Nazgûl's winged steed, panics and falls, crushing the king beneath him. Dernhelm and Merry are left to face the contemptuous Nazgûl, who boasts,

> "No living man can hinder me!"
>
> Then Merry heard of all sounds in that hour the strangest. It seemed that Dernhelm laughed, and the clear voice was like the ring of steel. "But no living man am I! You look upon a woman. Éowyn I am, Éomund's daughter...."
>
> The winged creature screamed at her, but the Ringwraith was silent, as if in sudden doubt.[2]

Merry, moreover, is not a man but a hobbit. The Ringwraith has fallen victim to the false confidence inspired by prophecy—there is always a catch. Merry manages to cut the Nazgûl's Achilles' tendon and Éowyn decapitates him, but both are wounded in body and by the Black Breath.

At this point, ships of the Corsairs of Umbar, Sauron's allies, sail up the river, but just as it seems that the forces of evil have received reinforcements, the ships unfurl the standard of Aragorn. It is he and the Rangers, with Gimli and Legolas, and the battle resumes.

While all of this is happening, Denethor—deluded by biased visions sent from Sauron in a *palantír*—prepares to die. Gandalf manages to save Faramir, but Denethor goes to his death in delusion. In the Houses of Healing, Aragorn proves his kingship (for the true king is a healer as well as a warrior) by healing Merry, Faramir, and Éowyn with *athelas*. The shattered remnants of the Fellowship are reunited.

Thereupon, Aragorn and the leaders of the allied armies decide to advance on the gates of Mordor. There, the emissary of Sauron shows them

Sam's sword, Frodo's *mithril* (truesilver) shirt, and an elven cloak, suggest-ing (but never stating) they have been captured. Gandalf demands to see Frodo and Sam themselves, whom Sauron's lieutenant will not produce. Battle begins, and Pippin finds himself in the thick of it. Buried under the corpse of a troll, he loses consciousness just as he hears someone calling, "The Eagles are coming!" and his last thought is that this is just like the end of Bilbo's tale.

The sword, cloak, and *mithril* shirt had been taken by the orcs when they captured Frodo, but Sam has managed to rescue his master. The two make their way, tortuously, across the Plateau of Gorgoroth, followed by Gollum. When they finally reach the Cracks of Doom, however, Frodo claims the Ring as his own, refusing to destroy it. Gollum will not sit still while his Precious is claimed by another; he bites the Ring from Frodo's finger and, in his gleeful caperings at this reunion, tumbles into Doom. The Ring is destroyed.

With the destruction of Sauron and all his works, the Third Age has ended. Aragorn reclaims his throne and marries his love, Arwen. The hobbits make their way back to the Shire, but the story is not yet over: Saruman has escaped the Ents and taken over the hobbits' homeland, turning it into a modernist nightmare. The returning hobbits rout "Sharkey" and his minions, and Saruman finally dies of a knife in the back delivered by Wormtongue. As the new age finally consolidates, ev-eryone settles down except for Frodo, still tormented by his Nazgûl wound. The destruction of Sauron means that the age of the elves has also passed; Frodo—and Bilbo—finally depart for the Grey Havens with the last boatload of elves, which also carries Gandalf beyond the world of men.

THE EVIL OF DREAD

The primary concern of *The Lord of the Rings* is a battle against evil, which has many shapes and faces. The first sign of evil is the arrival of the Nazgûl in the Shire. The Nazgûl grow in threat and horror throughout *The Lord of the Rings*. At first they are merely sinister figures, hooded and horsed, asking innocuous questions about "Bagginsss." Dark as they may be, they appear to be in the dark themselves, for they are uncertain which Baggins they seek, Bilbo or Frodo.

Tolkien reveals the nature of the Nazgûl slowly. Gandalf first mentions them while describing the history of the Rings of Power: "It is many years since the Nine walked abroad. Yet who knows? As the Shadow grows once more, so they too may walk again."[3] The first Black Rider questions

Gaffer Gamgee, and Frodo, overhearing the conversation, can only hear clearly Gaffer's side of the exchange; the Rider is only a strange and unpleasant sound. When Frodo finally sees the Rider himself, his visual appearance is only slightly alarming—his real menace seems to arise from the fact that he seems to be tracking the hobbits by smell, like a predatory animal. Also, Frodo, for the first time, feels the compulsion to put on the Ring against his will. Next, Farmer Maggot tells the hobbits that he has spoken with a Rider: The Rider scared off Maggot's dog, he sat unnaturally still on his horse and moved stiffly, his voice was queer and hissing, and his hood hid his face (or lack thereof).

Although the Black Riders are obviously a menace, the connection between them and the Nine is not yet evident. They ask questions—questions the hobbits would prefer not be answered—but they take no action until Bree, when the hobbits' room is vandalized and their ponies driven off. The same night, they later learn, Fatty Bolger was attacked by another band of Nazgûl at Frodo's house back in the Shire. It is not until the group reaches Weathertop that the hobbits understand that the Riders and the Nine are the same; Frodo succumbs to their siren call to put on the Ring, and finally he perceives the true nature of the Riders with his Ring-enhanced senses.

The Nazgûl are indeed men, kings who accepted Rings of Power from Sauron and became corrupted. The Nazgûl are literally "stretched thin," so thin that they no longer appear to have any physical presence at all. They are not quite ghosts, but no longer men.

In addition to being dangerous enemies, therefore, the Nazgûl provide a warning of what happens to someone who accepts one of Sauron's rings, even a relatively low-power ring. Furthermore, after Frodo is wounded by the Nazgûl's dagger at Weathertop, the dagger tip in his shoulder and the wound it leaves even after it is removed bind him dangerously to the Nazgûl. This wound will cast its shadow over the rest of Frodo's life, causing him to fall ill every year on the anniversary of receiving it (perhaps a reference to Tolkien's own interminable relapses from trench fever). This alien evil that invades the Shire turns out to be a disturbingly intimate enemy.

THE EVIL OF PERSUASION

It takes no great powers of perception to realize that the Nazgûl are evil. Saruman's evil is more subtle—and therefore more easy to hide. In his presentation of the Ents, Tolkien has presented one half of an equation: good = nature (or organic creation). Saruman represents the other half: bad = machine (or mechanical creation). For Tolkien, machinery is creation for the sake of destructive power, as opposed to art (or sub-creation), which is creation for the sake of constructive beauty. Throughout *The Lord of the Rings*, there are references to Saruman's interest in machines, in mechanical doodads; "He has a mind of metals and wheels," as Treebeard says disapprovingly.[4] His name even derives from Old English *searu*, which means "device, contrivance, design, art (in the sense of making things)." He is also disturbingly "modern"; as T. A. Shippey points out,[5] he talks like a policeman or politician, whose idols are Law, Order, and Rule, which means "You do what I tell you to do." This "modernity" is very different from Bilbo's bourgeois approach to contractual negotiation in *The Hobbit*. Bilbo may show himself to be interested in luxury rather than adventure, but his aim is to have things understood and agreed upon openly; Saruman's intention is to mislead and obfuscate.

Saruman is so persuasive that following his orders is a pleasure. The sound of his voice makes the meaning of his words irrelevant, much like the seductive voice of the dragon Smaug. This power of creation—the creation of a desire to please, of a willingness to carry out orders—is the closest thing to a spell found in *The Lord of the Rings*, an en-*chant*-ment that creates a false consciousness through the sound of the voice.

For all Saruman's honeyed words, however, it is no coincidence that Gríma, his most loyal servant, is known as Wormtongue. Gríma's verbal power is not as strong as his master's, and therefore his intentions are more self-evident. When Gríma accuses Gandalf of lying, Gandalf replies, "That word comes too oft and too easy from your lips,"[6] implying that Gríma accuses others of lying so readily because he himself lies. Saruman's corruption lies in his becoming the servant of another—Sauron—and in losing his independence, he also seems to lose some of his linguistic power. When Saruman tells the men of Rohan that he alone can help them, Gimli replies, "The words of this wizard stand on their heads.... In the language of Orthanc, help means ruin, and saving means slaying, that is plain."[7] Saruman's words are like campaign promises or a sales pitch, and once the mark is aware of his duplicity, his ability to charm is lessened. Sauron's evil is on an epic scale, a peril to the soul, but Saruman's evil is somehow more familiar to modern readers, because it is the voice of expedience, urging people to do what they want rather than what is right. It is significant that Saruman's exposure takes place in the open air and in daylight. His power is a machine-made power, but the power of nature, of trees—the Ents and the Huorns—has torn apart his war machines and his battlements. His spell has come to an end.

EVIL ON THE MOUNTAIN

Tolkien's depictions of evil become increasingly complex throughout his epic. Initial assumptions of black and white dichotomies are greyed down. (Is it a coincidence that Frodo's final destination is the Grey Havens?) Nowhere is this seen more clearly than in the character of Gollum. He is evil, he is untrustworthy, he is a murderer and a liar, he is creepy, and yet he is finally not a figure of horror but of pity. Gollum's role in the final destruction of the Ring is the payback for the pity that has stayed the hands of everyone who has the chance and the justification to kill him. Even Sam, the most reluctant to exculpate Gollum, finally realizes what a wretched creature he is, how he is driven by a force infinitely more strong than he is that will only crush him in the end. The fact that Gollum is pitiable does not, however, make him guiltless. Tolkien does not believe that victimization is a blanket excuse for all sins committed under its influence.

Gollum's end may be Tolkien's answer to the question of the role of Evil in God's creation. Even before acquiring the Ring, Gollum was weak and sneaky; he murdered his best friend to get the Ring and is willing to murder again to recover it; even when he begins to remember what goodness is, he chooses betrayal instead. Gollum chooses evil unambiguously out of his own free will, and the fact that evil is increasingly easy to choose once he is in the Ring's thrall is no excuse for making those choices, it just means that he has made it harder and harder to do the right thing, which is still the right thing. Thus, although Gollum inadvertently acts as an agent for good when his tumbling into the Cracks of Doom with the Ring in his hand destroys Sauron and all his works, and also saves Frodo from the consequences of claiming the Ring, Gollum's act grew out of an evil impulse: He wanted the Ring, and he took it. Even if the only thing he wants from its power is to have fresh fish from the sea three times a day, his lust for that power causes him to break all the laws of the social contract.

Tolkien seems to present two reasons why God allows evil in the world. First, evil is necessary for the operation of free will, since if there is only one choice—good—there is no choice. Second, however, it seems that ultimately, evil is self-defeating. Good can fight evil, and must fight evil, but the madnesses and lusts that evil arouses end up at cross-purposes. The purpose of good fighting evil seems to be not so much that good will necessarily triumph, but that good's delaying action provides enough time for evil to defeat itself: The insane desire of one small, hobbitlike Gollum can confound the vast, destructive works of Sauron.

EVIL ON THE HOME FRONT

The destruction of Sauron and all his works is a defeat of evil on a grand scale, but the story of *The Lord of the Rings* has been told from the point of view of the little guy. Even though it would seem that the heroes should be able to return home to peace and contentment, when the hobbits reach the Shire, they discover another Wasteland in the making. The provinces are always something behind the times, and Saruman is not out of the picture yet. The chapter "The Scouring of the Shire" has been seen as Tolkien's commentary on communism, fascism, Nazism, or a "paternalistic, reactionary, anti-intellectual, racist, fascistic, and, perhaps worst of all in contemporary terms, irrelevant" world-view.[8] However, these interpretations look at the chapter from the point of view of modernist literary form. This kind of final episode, seemingly irrelevant to the main theme of the main story according to modern literary sensibilities, is actually quite common in medieval narrative. While some scholars dismiss these episodes as bad construction on the part of the author or bad transmission on the part of the scribe, others suggest that these episodes may have been seen as integral parts of the story, although there is still no consensus on why. One possibility is that the capping episode served as a kind of mini-sequel, a reflection of the ongoing nature of reality beyond the limits of "the story." It may also be a way to incorporate important elements of oral tradition that did not fit into the main story. Finally, the capping episode may have been a metaphorical restatement of the main themes of the story; oral narrative needs to repeat its message in order to be sure that the audience, who is listening rather than reading, understands it.

"The Scouring of the Shire" is usually seen as evidence of Tolkien's "antiegalitarianism," reflected in the fact that the heroism of *The Lord of the Rings* is associated with noble lineage. Sauron and Saruman are seen as overseeing the only "egalitarian" societies in Middle-earth, which is taken as a sign that Tolkien thought democracy was evil. Yet this "egalitarianism" simply consists of everyone being equally enslaved, profits and power going to a terrorist elite. There is no real egalitarianism in the Shire under Saruman, there is simply the rhetoric of egalitarianism, much like George Orwell's Newspeak in his novel *1984* (1949). Tolkien was a conservative—a real conservative. One gets the sense that even capitalism was too newfangled for him. For Tolkien, evil did not lie in social stratification but in taking profits from the land rather than "husbanding" it.

Another aspect of "The Scouring of the Shire" that is missed from a purely modernist perspective is how it fits into the medieval pattern of the journey to the Otherworld. One of the expected results of such a journey is that the hero brings back some kind of "good" to benefit his society, a treasure or some kind of new knowledge. For hobbits, any journey outside the Shire is a journey to the Otherworld (just as in medieval Welsh narrative, a journey to Ireland or England is a journey to the Otherworld). On their return to the Shire, the hobbits bring back the news of the return of the king, and use the skills they have learned in the "Otherworld" to return their world to its previous balance.

The scouring of the Shire provides Merry and Pippin with the opportunity to exhibit their new status—their new "stature." When they left, they were feckless youths; now they have not only become battle-tested warriors, but they also served as the catalysts of change for three different peoples: the Ents, the Rohirrim, and the Gondorians. Together, they incited a forest to march. Merry's hobbitness was the reason he was able to help slay the Lord of the Nazgûl, and Pippin prevented Faramir from being killed by his father. Even Sam, who is not markedly changed by his adventures, returns to gain a new status, using his gift from Galadriel to replant the Shire and ending up as Mayor. These three contrast with Frodo, who is faded and diminished by his efforts. Some quests may ask just too much of the quester; evil can never be completely eradicated.

NOTES

1. J. R. R. Tolkien, *The Return of the King* (Boston: Houghton Mifflin, 1956), 48.

2. *Return of the King*, 116.

3. J. R. R. Tolkien, *The Fellowship of the Ring* (Boston: Houghton Mifflin, 1954), 60–61.

4. J. R. R. Tolkien, *The Two Towers* (Boston: Houghton Mifflin, 1955), 76.

5. T. A. Shippey, *The Road to Middle-earth* (Boston: Houghton Mifflin, 1983), 128–30.

6. *Two Towers*, 125.

7. *Two Towers*, 184.

8. Walter Scheps, "The Fairy-tale Morality of *The Lord of the Rings*," in *A Tolkien Compass*, edited by Jared Lobdell (La Salle, Ill.: Open Court Publishing, 1975), 52.

Chapter 10

DOUBLES AND KINGS

One of Tolkien's most common narrative techniques is to create "doubles," pairs of characters who, through similarity and contrast, express alternative approaches or solutions to a problem so that the right choice can be made. Many critics who have denounced Tolkien's "simplistic" characterizations have overlooked the fact that the simplicity of the characters only persists as long as the characters are viewed in isolation: Their complexity and philosophical subtlety can be appreciated only in context. This is a technique that Tolkien learned from his immersion in medieval literature, which operates on many of the same premises.

OLD AND NEW HOBBITS

Gollum—probably the most complex character in *The Lord of the Rings*, certainly the most psychologically tortured—is his own double. Gollum and his alter ego, Sméagol, constitute an evil and dangerous character who comes close to redemption, but not close enough.

In *The Hobbit*, Gollum is deceitful and tricky, but even then Bilbo's riddles kindle memories of "days when he had been less lonely and sneaky and nasty."[1] Memories of happier days only serve to make him irritable, however, and the more he recalls what is good in him and in the world, the more he recoils into evil actions. This originally simple dichotomy within his character widens until it develops into a split personality: Gollum (dominated by the Ring) and Sméagol (the remnant of his original unpleasant but uncorrupt personality), what Sam calls Stinker and Slinker. Frodo soon realizes that it is possible to tell which personality is dominant by which personal pronouns he uses: Sméagol refers to himself in the singular, while Gollum, the second personality to develop, refers to himself in the plural (i.e., himself and Sméagol).

Gollum's "doubleness" predates his split personality, however. The Ring was originally discovered by Sméagol's friend, Déagol. This rhyming or alliterating naming pattern, Sméagol/Déagol, is typical of mythological twins and doubles—in fact, Tolkien had already used it in the naming of the dwarves in *The Hobbit,* where the names were taken directly from a list in the Edda. The Ring corrupts Sméagol by inciting him to kill his "double." Gollum claims that the Ring should have been his because it was his birthday, and it proves also to be the day when "Gollum" is born.

Frodo sees several examples of the Ring's corrupting power—the Nazgûl show what happens to those who accept rings from Sauron, and Boromir shows what desire for the Ring's power can lead to—but the Ring's effect on Gollum is more disturbing because he is so much closer to being a hobbit. Gandalf warns Frodo that the Ring bestows power in accordance with the natural power of the one who holds it; hobbits are small, provincial, domestic creatures. Aside from inciting Gollum to kill in order to possess it, the Ring makes him shun the sun and burrow as far underground as he can go. The Ring can grant him all the power in the world, yet Gollum's vision of what will happen when he regains his Precious is pitifully simple: "See, my precious: If we has it, then we can escape, even from Him, eh? Perhaps we grows very strong, stronger than Wraiths. Lord Sméagol? Gollum the Great? *The* Gollum! Eat fish every day, three times a day, fresh from the Sea."[2] For all his evil, the most Gollum can envision is eating well and not being bullied. (Notice that in naming this powerful creature, he first thinks of calling himself Sméagol but quickly switches to Gollum.)

Sméagol finds this vision attractive, but his desire for the Ring is tempered by his desire to help someone who has been kind to him—Frodo. Although Frodo has made him swear by his Precious to assist the hobbits, Sméagol's willingness to help Frodo (and *not* Sam) seems to derive at least in part from Frodo's kindness in taking the elf rope off of Sméagol's leg and speaking nicely to him. Sméagol's trust in Frodo as an individual overrides his hatred for hobbits in general and Bagginses in particular. Ironically, Frodo gains his compassion for Gollum/Sméagol as a result of their shared experience of being Ringbearers; he understands the pull the Ring exercises over its bearer. Thus, Gollum is not only a double in himself, but he is also a double of Frodo (and of Bilbo). His mental fragmentation shows how Frodo could potentially split, too, with his hobbit personality trapped within the corrupt, Ring-born personality.

Gollum/Sméagol is split between the desire for complete self-reliance and for connection with others. Gollum's journey through the Dead Marshes to Cirith Ungol forces him into such connection for the first time in over five hundred years. After all, ever since he acquired the Ring, his only connection with others has consisted of these people torturing him (from his point of view) for information about the Ring. Yet nonetheless, as soon as he is shown even a scrap of kindness by Frodo, Sméagol emerges, perhaps another example of the toughness and stamina of hobbit-kind. Yet even though Sméagol stubbornly lives on in Gollum's inner core, he is not strong enough to overcome the desire for the Ring that leads Gollum to betray Sam and Frodo to Shelob.

As already noted, at the beginning of *The Fellowship of the Ring,* Tolkien's narrative point of view was chiefly located in Frodo; with the breaking of the Fellowship, the point of view is also shattered, but usually lies with a hobbit. Sam's point of view has been presented on occasion, but mostly as a change of pace. In the second subsection of *The Two Towers,* however, Sam comes to the fore as Frodo recedes. Tolkien often stated that Sam was based on the working-class soldiers he had known in World War I, whom he felt had been the true heroes of a mismanaged war. Tolkien conceived the major theme of *The Lord of the Rings* to be the importance of the small and overlooked, the "ignoble," in the grand scheme of things: "[W]ithout the high and noble the simple and vulgar is utterly mean; and without the simple and ordinary the noble and heroic is meaningless."[3] Tolkien presents events from the point of view of the simple and ordinary, and as the challenges of the quest make Frodo increasingly "noble," the point of view shifts from him to the very ordinary Sam.

Unlike Bilbo, who did not realize that there was going to be a problem transporting his payment home until he reached Smaug's treasure horde, Frodo suspects from the beginning that he will not survive his quest, and he becomes reconciled to his fate. But this also makes him a less satisfactory consciousness for the narrative point of view. It is hard to empathize with a protagonist who has lost all hope of survival. Sam's consciousness becomes the narrative point of view in large part because Sam is not as wise and saintly as Frodo. Sam also expresses the less noble emotions and concerns that Frodo will not admit—not only dislike and distrust of Gollum, but also the practical concerns of food and sleep. Although Sam is the epitome of the loyal servant, he also shows the limitations of his role. He is indiscreet; he is mistrustful; he is a little jealous of the compassion Frodo shows towards Gollum; and at the crucial moment, he makes the wrong decision about the Ring.

Even though Sam's intentions are good, his choice to take the Ring when Frodo appears to be dead shows how deadly good intentions can be where the Ring is concerned. Sam's loyalty has always been to Frodo alone; he has little understanding of the stakes in the quest and has come along simply to care for his master. The Ring, however, has a kind of sentience that causes those around it to act in ways that will advance the Ring's agenda at the expense of their own. Gandalf, in particular, thinks it cannot have been coincidence that brought Bilbo to Gollum's underground lake at precisely the right moment to pick up the Ring, when it was increasingly clear that Gollum was never going to leave the mountain. The Ring's power influences Sam to make a decision in the best interests of the Ring—taking it from a disabled Bearer—instead of sticking by his master, Frodo, but this crucial misstep gives Sam his own chance to become truly heroic. Putting on the Ring—always a dangerous action—allows him to discover his mistake by overhearing the orcs, and as soon as he knows that Frodo is alive, he realizes that he has made a mistake, all his intention turns back to his loyalty towards his master, and the Ring's power over him fades. Frodo, under the Ring's sway for a longer time, is not as resilient.

BOROMIR AND FARAMIR

Boromir, the son of Denethor, is one of the most ambivalent characters in *The Lord of the Rings*. He is brave and his intentions are good, but he is also prone to pride and arrogance. He makes sure everyone knows that his city and his soldiers have borne the brunt of holding back the forces of Mordor; in contrast, Aragorn accepts the fact that his own and the Rangers' efforts will not be acknowledged by those who most benefit from them. The fact that Boromir's brother is the one who had repeated prophetic dreams of the return of the Sword that was Broken (which is carried by Aragorn, the rightful king of Gondor), while Boromir dreamed it only once, yet he is the one who has come to discover its meaning, is the first hint that there may be some problem with Boromir and power. From the very start, he seems to have a bias, if well intentioned, towards usurpation; this bodes ill for his acceptance of Aragorn as the rightful king.

Boromir represents the extreme of the heroic ethos: He is a protector and a leader; he has faith in his mental and physical powers, and he trusts the evidence of his own senses. He is loyal to his own people and a dangerous enemy. Yet his heroic stature is the source of his downfall. He protects and leads because he considers others incapable of protecting or leading themselves; he trusts his own experience but therefore is unwilling to accept anyone else's word; he sees the world in black and white, Us and Them. He is a practical man, but he cannot cope with magic—and magic is Sauron's most potent weapon.

As soon as Boromir learns of the Ring's power, he wants to use it to destroy Sauron: "Let the Ring be your weapon, if it has such power as you say. Take it, and go forth to victory!"[4] Although Elrond and Gandalf tell him that the Ring will corrupt anyone who wields it, Boromir doubts them because *he* has never betrayed anyone, so how could he do so under the influence of a ring of metal? Yet already he is influenced by the promise of the Ring's power and the desire to use the Ring is planted in his heart. Since Elrond, Gandalf, and Aragorn—the people he considers to be his superiors, the only ones he would yield to in precedence—have repudiated its use, once Frodo has refused to use it, Boromir finds it easy to convince himself that he has the right to it. He, of course, would only use it for good.

Boromir is not wholly evil, not even mostly evil. He helps the smaller members of the Fellowship when they are snowed in on Caradhras, he fights valiantly against the orcs in Moria, and he dies attempting to protect Merry and Pippin from yet another onslaught of orcs. And Boromir's madness provides Frodo with the impetus to separate himself from the Fellowship. Seeing the Ring's corrupting effects on an undeniably heroic man forces him to the realization that he must bear his burden alone. Although Boromir is finally betrayed by his own blindness to the limitations of his heroic ethos, his fall kindles a truer heroism in Frodo, who carries on his quest well-warned of his own frailties. Furthermore, by leaving his companions, Frodo forces Aragorn to follow his own destiny to Gondor.

While Gollum and Sméagol represent the strengths and weaknesses inherent in hobbits, Boromir and Faramir represent the strengths and weaknesses of men. Boromir in himself exhibited the limitations of the heroic ideal of the warrior; Faramir shows how those qualities can be brought to a higher level with the addition of some wizardly wisdom and teaching.

Even before Faramir arrives on the scene, there are hints that he is the more mystical brother, prone to prophetic dreams. He also has a vision of seeing Boromir's funeral boat, with Boromir's corpse surrounded by an unearthly light. Faramir is not just a visionary, but an accomplished warrior, if not as single-minded as his brother. Boromir is a career soldier, pure and simple, while Faramir is more in the mold of the sportsman-scholar (an ideal still alive in Tolkien's youth, though the relic of a vanished age today).

Faramir's tale of the failure of the kings of Gondor and their replacement by their stewards echoes the decline of the Merovingian kings of France (who reigned from 476 to 750). Their stewards, known as Mayors of the Palace, slowly became the de facto governors of the Frankish realm.

Eventually one of the stewards, Pepin III, dethroned the last Merovingian king, Childeric III, initiating the Carolingian dynasty (named after Pepin's grandson, Charlemagne). When Boromir asked his father, "How many hundreds of years needs it to make a steward a king, if the king returns not?" Denethor's reported response was: "Few years, maybe, in other places of less royalty. In Gondor ten thousand years would not suffice."[5] The stewards of Gondor are in the same position as the early Carolingians: Governing power is theirs, but are they legitimate? The Carolingians got around it by initiating the ritual of papal anointment of the emperor (who thus became the "Holy Roman Emperor"), relocating the source of legitimacy from bloodline to religious authority. The stewards of Gondor have no such recourse, living in a world with no organized religion. However, it seems to be merely an accident of circumstances that has kept Boromir on the straight and narrow all his life; he has not yet fallen merely because he has not been tempted. Faramir, however, is given the same opportunity to take the Ring for himself, and resists.

THÉODEN AND DENETHOR

The most significant pair that Tolkien presents may well be his pair of kings, presenting contrasting models of rule. Neither, ultimately, is completely sufficient, but both must be presented in order that Aragorn's actions and decisions may be placed in a proper context, so that his apotheosis as the first king of the Fourth Age can be appreciated. Tolkien offers two examples of elderly leaders in *The Lord of the Rings:* Théoden of Rohan and Denethor of Minas Tirith. Both are being undermined—sapped—by the Enemy, Théoden worn down by the poisonous words of Gríma Wormtongue, and Denethor deceived by the false images he sees in his *palantír.*

When Théoden is first seen, he is bent and depends on a staff for support; he sits indoors in a dark hall, brooding. Gandalf's first move in his spiritual healing of Théoden is to force him into the light and air of the day, where Théoden's first comment is, "It is not so dark here."[6] The truly transforming act, however, is taking a sword once more in his hand and crying the battle call of the Rohirrim.

Théoden is suffering from depression, and his cure lies in throwing off the lethargy of depression for action, fresh air, and straight talk. Gandalf's healing magic is little more than common sense. Théoden's strength is still there, forced inward and downward by Wormtongue's deceptive counsel, and all he has to do to regain it is stand up straight and get some air in his lungs. As soon as Théoden's head has cleared, he sees for himself the sense of Gandalf's advice, which is only what all of his friends and family have been urging him to do all along. This act of walking from inside to outside in the act of healing is reversed, later, when Denethor, in his madness, moves from outside to inside, attempting to burn not only himself but his ailing son on a funeral pyre.

If it seems that there is something too simplistic about Théoden's cure, it is important that this cure through contact with nature occurs simultaneously with Merry and Pippin rousing the Ents. The Fellowship, no longer committed to accompanying Frodo to Mordor, is instead acting to rouse up the older generation, which has fallen into complacency and senile depression, under the delusion that the world is no longer their concern. The hobbits get the trees on the move, while the wizard works on the men. But also, Théoden's cure is to regain contact with the natural world. Tolkien here draws on the concept, typical of Indo-European mythology, that the king's role is to maintain the cosmic balance of the natural world.

The coming of a new king requires the passing of the old rule. The deaths of Théoden and Denethor are sad but necessary to clear the way for the new order. The manners of their deaths, however, provide another set of doubles that illustrate the strengths and weaknesses of the status quo. Both men have fallen victim to the lies of Sauron. Théoden is aware that his day is passing and has no more interest in the world or what happens to it. Denethor believes that he could continue to have an active role in the new world, were he not surrounded by traitors.

Each man has an heir, Éomer and Faramir, who patrols their territory and sends strangers to the capital for the ruler's judgement; both Éomer and Faramir encounter members of the Fellowship and decide to assist the strangers and let them continue their business. (Aragorn and Frodo each fill the function of the leader of the band of strangers who tests the heir.) In each case, the heir has to make a decision that is perceived by the ruler as a usurpation of his privilege, and in truth, these younger men are indeed making their first steps as rulers in making these decisions.

Théoden throws Éomer into prison, but when his mind is cleared by Gandalf, his first action is to release Éomer, recognizing that Éomer had made the right decision. Furthermore, once Théoden regains his self-confidence as a ruler, he is no longer threatened by his nephew's independence and indeed acknowledges that a good ruler is not one who keeps all power in his own hands and sticks to the letter of the law, but one who realizes that his own power derives from being able to delegate to trustworthy lieutenants. Théoden knows that his time may be short, but once the malice of Wormtongue is dissipated, he also knows that there is no reason why he should not be active until the very end and accepts the transition of power as a natural element of the transition from life to death.

Denethor's reactions are very different. He berates Faramir for not bringing him the Ring and wishes it were Faramir who were dead rather than Boromir. He does not imprison his son but sends him out on a potentially fatal mission. When Faramir is wounded, Denethor does not wait until he is dead to set his funeral pyre. Denethor may live and sleep in his armor, ever ready for war, but when the crisis arrives, he caves in without even the pretense of a fight. If he cannot have it his way, he will have none at all, and neither will anyone else.

Théoden's recuperation brings his people together and minimizes their losses in the war—the civilians are sent to safety, and the only warriors to die, die in battle. Denethor not only kills himself—and nearly his son— but he also forces good men like Beregond to commit murder. It might also be argued that Denethor's self-immolation makes Théoden's death inevitable, for the crisis of Denethor's madness diverts Gandalf from the battlefield, where he had intended to draw the Nazgûl's fire, to the mortuary, where he must save Faramir.

Although they never meet, Denethor and Théoden are united by their passing. Once they have gone, their positions pass to the two heirs who had aroused their wrath, Faramir and Éomer. These two, moreover, will be united by ties of kinship with the marriage of Éowyn, Éomer's sister, to Faramir.

LIVING AND DEAD

Although Aragorn's return as the king marks the end of the Third Age, it sometimes seems that most of his story has taken place offstage, before this epic began. In a sense, his regaining of his birthright is tangential to the quest to destroy the Ring: He and Frodo are both working against the same enemy, but Frodo simply needs to destroy the Ring—one action, difficult as it may be to achieve—while Aragorn's task requires not only prowess but politics. Once Frodo has destroyed the Ring, his task is over, but Aragorn's is just beginning. In order to become the king of the living, however, Aragorn first must prove that he can master the dead.

Aragorn's challenge both parallels and contrasts with Gandalf's transformation. As with Gandalf's death and rebirth in the abyss of Moria, the Paths of the Dead are yet another passage underneath a mountain. Throughout Tolkien's novels, underneath the mountain is where death lives—the undead Gollum, the dead civilization of Moria, the foresworn dead. Unlike Gandalf, who battles the figure of death—the Balrog—and defeats it, Aragorn offers the dead the chance to redeem themselves and become truly dead, rather than restless spirits. He has to risk himself and his men, for these spirits drive men mad, and if he has miscalculated, he loses everything. Furthermore, when Gandalf fell into the abyss, the Balrog took him against his will in a fight; when Aragorn traverses the Paths of the Dead, he does it of his own free will, of his own choosing. The Dead Men of Dunharrow had sworn to support Gondor at the end of the Second Age, but they had turned to Sauron in the crunch. The Battle of the Five Armies that concludes *The Hobbit* is a battle among dwarves, elves, men, orcs, and wargs—all the humanlike races of Middle-earth. Although the overthrow of Isengard is achieved by Ents and Huorns, and the Huorns tidy up the pickings from the Battle of Helm's Deep, the War of the Ring is primarily a war of men against men and orcs. The representatives of the other races are merely token forces. By giving the Dead Men a chance to redeem themselves, Aragorn also eliminates them, beginning the task of clearing the boards of the supernatural and nonhuman remnants from the previous ages and focusing the coming age on mortal men.

At the same time, proving that he has power over the dead—that he can summon them and they will come to his aid—proves that Aragorn is ready to become king. Although there is no organized religion in *The Lord of the Rings*, Tolkien made it clear in The Silmarillion that there had been worship of God in Númenor, and that the kings of Númenor were priest-kings. (The faint echo of that religion is seen in the Gondorian practice of facing the west—where the Númenorian temple had been—before eating.) As a general rule, priest-kings are believed to echo in their persons the order of the whole cosmos—when the king is healthy, wise, and fruitful, the land is fruitful, too. This connection between king and land is also the source of the belief that the true king is a healer—as he can harmonize nature and culture by his connection with the land, he can harmonize the warring influences within an ailing body by his touch. As the microcosmos, the rightful king also has power over the land and under the land. By summoning the dead, Aragorn risks becoming one of the dead himself, but by doing it successfully, he shows that he is the rightful king.

NOTES

1. *Hobbit*, 70.
2. *Two Towers*, 241.
3. Carpenter, *Letters*, 160.
4. *Fellowship of the Ring*, 281.
5. *Two Towers*, 278.
6. *Two Towers*, 120.

Chapter 11

FAME AND FORTUNE
(1955–1973)

Tolkien was sixty-two when *Lord of the Rings* was finally published, and after a lifetime of economic struggles, it was becoming clear that his unusual profit-sharing contract with Allen & Unwin was going to be quite remunerative. Each of the first two years that the books were in publication netted him more in royalties than his yearly salary as a professor. There was a radio adaptation of the trilogy on the BBC and preparations for translation into other languages (Dutch and Swedish the first). There were also overtures from Hollywood. In 1957, Tolkien was approached by a consortium of Morton Grady Zimmerman, Al Broadax (at the time executive producer of the Popeye television series, later to be one of the producers of the Beatles movie *Yellow Submarine,* 1968), and Forrest J. Ackerman (the man who invented the term "sci-fi" and a well-known figure in science fiction film and fandom). Tolkien was utterly unimpressed with their treatment for an animated version of *The Lord of the Rings,* which took a laissez-faire approach to the fine details of the plot that Tolkien considered key to his vision of Middle-earth. In a letter to Ackerman critiquing the treatment sent to him for comment, Tolkien makes the prescient comment that in the second two parts of the treatment, "It almost seems as if Z[immerman], having spent much time and work on Part I, now found himself short not only of space but of patience to deal with the two more difficult volumes . . . "[1] All subsequent attempts to consolidate *The Lord of the Rings* into a single movie were doomed to failure; it was not until Peter Jackson was able to obtain backing for three complete films, running a total of at least nine hours, that an adequate cinematic representation of Middle-earth could be achieved. However,

Hollywood was only willing to take such a large financial risk nearly fifty years after the books' publication, once they were established as true classics, and not a mere flash in the pan.

The first ten years after the publication of *Lord of the Rings* saw Tolkien established as a popular but quirky author. His sales were solid and steady, but he was still what might be considered a niche-market writer. He received many fan letters—one, indeed, from a real Sam Gamgee—and was extremely gracious in answering questions and expounding on his intentions and the underlying philosophy of his masterpiece. Meanwhile, his academic career was winding down. He was invited to give the inaugural O'Donnell lecture at Oxford—an annual lecture to be given on some aspect of the Celtic languages in English—in 1955, and presented his thoughts on "English and Welsh."[2] However, although he continued to assume that, with *Lord of the Rings* off his chest, he would now have time to write all the other things he "should" have been writing all these years, very little materialized. He still hoped to get The Silmarillion in publishable form, but his ineffable talents for perfectionism and procrastination prevented him from finishing it to his satisfaction. (Christopher Tolkien finally managed to edit the manuscript pieces into publishable form after his father had died.)

Tolkien retired from his professorship in 1959, at the age of sixty-seven, and prepared to settle in to a happy and well-cushioned retirement. Edith, who was three years his elder, had always had health problems, and as she got older, she became increasingly lame and prone to digestive troubles. Tolkien devoted most of his time to caring for her in their Headington house. Unfortunately, the house was two miles from Oxford and the nearest bus stop was farther than Edith could comfortably walk, requiring a taxi whenever she wanted to go somewhere. Even though money was not an issue, the trouble of making arrangements was often too much, and the two simply stayed at home, alone. They were in a fair way to becoming an isolated senior citizen couple.

Tolkien's estrangement from C. S. Lewis became complete in the late 1950's, when Lewis married an American divorcee, Joy Gresham. Tolkien had turned a more or less blind eye to Lewis's peculiar relationship with Mrs. Moore, who died in January 1951, nearly eighty and out of her mind. Partly this had been possible because Mrs. Moore stayed firmly at The Kilns and did not intrude on the all-male society of Oxford and the Inklings. Lewis wanted his new wife, whom he had married when she was believed to be virtually on her deathbed with cancer, only to go into miraculous remission, to be part of his social life precisely at the time when Tolkien was increasingly lacking in all-male companionship. When

Lewis died, unexpectedly young, on November 22, 1963 (a passing over-shadowed by the assassination of President John F. Kennedy on the same day), Tolkien refused to write his obituary or to contribute to a memorial volume of essays. Nonetheless, he attended the funeral and had a mass said for him, perhaps his final retaliation for Lewis's conversion to the "wrong" Christianity twenty-some years previously.

THE BIRTH OF A CULT

In 1965, it came to the attention of Allen & Unwin, and their Ameri-can counterparts Houghton Mifflin, that an unauthorized paperback edi-tion of *The Lord of the Rings* was in preparation by Ace Books, a well-known science-fiction paperback publisher. Ace claimed that Houghton Mifflin had contravened American copyright laws by import-ing more than the allowed number of unbound sheets (to be bound into book format in the United States) from the United Kingdom; this, theo-retically, voided Houghton Mifflin's copyright and put *The Lord of the Rings* in public domain. Since the point of a pirated edition is to avoid paying royalties to the author, they were able to produce the volumes for seventy-five cents apiece (considerably less than the hardcover price). Tolkien's stories were beginning to gain a reputation on college campuses, and 100,000 copies of the unauthorized paperback sold in 1965.

Meanwhile, Allen & Unwin and Houghton Mifflin realized that the only way they could get control of the property again would be to publish their own paperback, but in order to do so, they needed to publish a "re-vised" edition that was not identical to what Ace was publishing. This, of course, required Tolkien to revise—always a dangerous proposition. In fact, not completely understanding the financial importance of the situ-ation, he began by working on revisions to *The Hobbit,* which was not in any danger. Finally, in late 1965, the "authorized" paperback, published by Ballantine Books, hit the bookstores. Now, Tolkien's generosity in his painstaking responses to fan letters over the past decade began to pay off—all the more so as his fan base was expanding with the paperback publications. He took every opportunity of mentioning in his correspon-dences that the Ace edition of the books did not pay him royalties and urged his fans to purchase the Ballantine editions, even though they cost ninety-five cents to the Ace's seventy-five (twenty cents may not seem like much in today's book market, but it was, after all, a difference of 22 percent). Soon sales of the Ballantine edition exceeded one million, thanks to word-of-mouth among Tolkien's fans. Under pressure from the Science Fiction Writers of America organization, Ace finally agreed to pay Tolkien a royalty for each copy of their edition and not to reprint after their current stock ran out.

An unexpected side effect of this skirmish within the usually rarified environs of the book-publishing world was increased publicity for *The Lord of the Rings*. There are many possible reasons for the books' becoming popular precisely at this point in time: escapism as the war in Vietnam escalated, a fancy for all things British sparked by the Beatles, the "British invasion," and the hipness of Carnaby Street, an increased interest in environmental issues that chimed with Tolkien's own anti-industrialism, and a softening of dogmatic certainties about the "real world" as a result of experimentation with hallucinogenic drugs erasing the stigma of "fantasy." After an acid trip, magic and elves did not seem quite so outré any more—indeed, a writer in *Time* magazine commented in 1966 that "The hobbit habit seems to be almost as catching as LSD."[3] But perhaps the real appeal of *The Lord of the Rings* to a generation that was busy protesting every aspect of "the Establishment" lay in its little-guy point of view. For all its heroic portrayal of a (just) war, *The Lord of the Rings* gave a generation of antiwar protesters hope that the faceless powers of evil could be defeated by the powerless.

Tolkien was somewhat bemused by his elevation from eccentric Oxford don to culture hero. He knew that *he* liked his books; who were all these other people? How could they adore Middle-earth with no solid grounding in philology? And why were they calling him on the telephone at all hours of the day and night (apparently ignorant of the realities of time zones)? An article on the "Tolkien phenomenon" in the *Saturday Evening Post* in 1966 noted that Tolkien frequently voiced his contempt for the various scholarly theses about *The Lord of the Rings*, for example, considering most of them "rather vain efforts." (Tolkien approved of the alphabet-seekers and genealogists, on the other hand, finding their efforts part of an amusing game.) He also viewed with distaste the idea that he was some kind of antiquated medievalist, burying himself in a fantasy world because he finds the present so unbearable. "My opinion of current affairs is not as depressed as some people's," he says. "I should say I'm a bit frightened that the Greeks hadn't got something in the saying that those whom the gods wish to destroy they first drive mad. Our modern world is like the tower of Babel—wild noise and confusion. But I think that a little history cures you. Living at the end of the sixteenth century would have been just as bad, but there weren't so many people around." He grants that "certain things that were good, were beautiful, were more nourishing to the human person" have been sacrificed to machines. "But I don't think you can refuse knowledge; I don't think there's a way out."[4]

THE LAST STAGE

By the beginning of 1968, the Tolkiens decided that it was time to move yet again. The house in Headington was too inconvenient for daily living, and it was too well known to unintentionally intrusive fans. Money was not an issue. So they settled in Bournemouth, a seaside town in the south of England. It was a town where Edith often vacationed, and she felt much more at ease there than in Oxford society. Bournemouth was full of retirees who liked to spend the day chatting about grandchildren and their small daily doings, toddling from breakfast to elevenses to lunch to tea to supper, taking walks by the sea and hiring cars to take them on the occasional excursion. Tolkien was not as entranced with Bournemouth as Edith was, but he realized that she was very happy in that milieu, and given that she had sacrificed her own social life for his academic advancement all those years in Oxford, he did not begrudge her the move. The Tolkiens purchased a small bungalow close to the Miramar hotel, where they had usually stayed on their vacations, and settled in happily. The single-story layout was perfect for Edith's mobility problems, and for the first time in their lives, they had central heating. Tolkien set himself up a study and began making a serious effort at setting The Silmarillion in order. Then, in the middle of November 1971, Edith fell ill with an inflamed gall bladder. She died at the age of eighty-two, on November 29.

Tolkien was shocked by the suddenness of Edith's death, but he also had reached the age when death was to be expected. When he had recovered from the immediate grief, his first order of business was to move back to Oxford. His old college, Merton, made him a residential honorary fellow, and for the first time since he was an undergraduate before World War I, Tolkien lived in rooms on the campus. He was given a set of rooms at 21 Merton Street, where a scout and his wife took care of him, and he ate his meals at the High Table and socialized in the Senior Common Room whenever he pleased. He visited his children and his brother Hilary (still a fruit farmer in Evesham), and he was made a Commander of the British Empire by Queen Elizabeth in 1973. More touchingly, in his opinion, he received an honorary doctorate of letters by Oxford in 1972, explicitly awarded for his work as a philologist rather than a novelist. He worked on The Silmarillion when he had the energy for it, but he also spent time talking about this work with Christopher, who had agreed to take over the task of completing The Silmarillion should Tolkien die before completing it.

He was, perhaps, prescient, or perhaps simply too old to fool himself any longer about his work habits. In any case, while on a visit to friends in Bournemouth at the end of August 1973, he was taken ill with a bleeding gastric ulcer that became complicated by a chest infection. He died on September 2, 1973, at the age of eighty-one.

THAT OLD GANG OF MINE

Tolkien's lasting influence as a writer would probably have surprised him—he knew that Middle-earth was important to him, but he did not quite understand why it would be important to other people. Part of his reputation, especially in the first twenty years or so after his death, was due to the mystique that grew up around the Inklings. Tolkien, especially in his later days, was inclined to play down their mutual influence, and C.S. Lewis had commented that Tolkien had "only two reactions to criticism. Either he begins the whole work over again from the beginning or else takes no notice at all."[5] What was important about the Inklings, however, was the interchange of ideas among a group of men who agreed that religion had a place in literature beyond simple devotional tracts and published sermons, but who wanted to express themselves in "genre fiction" rather than in "literary fiction."

The post–World War I era was not a golden age of fantasy until Tolkien and Lewis began publishing. After the late nineteenth century, when Tennyson made Arthuriana popular and William Morris's Arts and Crafts movement included a return to the preindustrial in literature as well as in home decor, the imaginations of "alternative" writers turned increasingly to the wonders of technology and of other planets. Science fiction replaced fantasy fiction.

The novels of Tolkien, Lewis, and Charles Williams present the seeds of the main trends in late-twentieth-century fantasy writing. Tolkien set the fashion for the creation of self-contained alternate worlds. The novelty of this can be seen in the fact that several reviewers of The Lord of the Rings thought that it took place on another planet. Lewis tried his hand at straightforward science fiction in his trilogy Out of the Silent Planet (1938), Perelandra (1943), and That Hideous Strength (1945), which took place on Mars and Venus, but was more famous for his journey-to-the-Otherworld children's series, the Chronicles of Narnia (1950–1956). Williams specialized in the "supernatural thriller," a hybrid of the mystery/thriller genre with fantasy. His novels did not have a huge influence during his own time, but they can now be seen as the seed of the "dark fantasy" subgenre that began to emerge in the 1990s.

Tolkien created self-contained worlds and used the natives of these worlds as his narrative point of view. Lewis wrote from the point of view of normal, contemporary individuals who encounter fantastic Other-worlds on other planets or in parallel universes. Williams wrote of a contemporary world and its mundane inhabitants, who are suddenly confronted with the intrusion of alternate realities into their own world. Tolkien and Lewis both based their fantasy worlds in the mythologies of medieval northern Europe; Lewis and Williams both made their reliance on Christian mythology explicit as well.

The Inklings put mysticism back in fantasy. Many of their literary disciples may have fallen into the habit of using magic as a *deus ex machina* the way that lesser sci-fi writers might over-rely on death rays and warp drives to skate over dubious plot points. However, for these three writers, the *deus* was really *Deus*, the Christian God who transcended mere science. Their heroes had to struggle, not only against monsters and magicians, but also with theological concepts of free will and predestination. Frodo is as much a Chosen One as Buffy the Vampire Slayer.

FROM SWORD AND SORCERY TO RING AND WIZARD

At the time Tolkien was writing, the closest thing to epic fantasy was the sword-and-sorcery fiction of Robert E. Howard's Conan the Barbarian stories (which he began publishing in the pulps in 1929). This genre took place in a world similar to Tolkien's Middle-earth, an impossibly ancient, mythic time populated by figures of myth and legend, but it concentrated on action and left philosophy far behind. Good was good, and was entitled to overcome evil, because evil was evil. It is hard to tell how familiar Tolkien was with this literature—he does say in a letter of 1968 that he reads a lot of "so-called Science Fiction and Fantasy,"[6] and he and Lewis would hardly have challenged each other to writing science fiction novels in the mid-1930s if they were not familiar with the genre, but Tolkien never drops names. The fact that Tolkien wanted to write a time-travel novel suggests that he was reading Conan-esque fiction and wanted to try his hand at it because he was dissatisfied with it (just as he wanted to rewrite the *Nibelungenlied* because he disliked Wagner's interpretation of the Germanic myths).

What Tolkien contributed to the sword-and-sorcery genre was a moral dimension. His heroes were not muscle-bound swordsmen, but little people who had to do their best with all the cards stacked against them and who might be damaged beyond recovery in the process, but who persisted because they had to. He added "coziness" to fantasy, the requirement of a self-consistent alternate world, and the awareness of multiple languages within that world. He also, less beneficially, added the concept of the 1,500-page trilogy, which in the hands of less accomplished writers often produced quantity rather than quality.

Under the influence of Gandalf, the wizard character in fantasy novels began to change. The archetypal wizard, the Merlin of Arthurian literature, had become a rather sedate character, a counselor to the king who used his magical talents for beneficent political ends. Tolkien's Gandalf, along with T. H. White's Merlin of *The Sword in the Stone* (1939), brought back some of the erratic madness of the original Welsh Myrddin, a tricksterlike poet-warrior of the sixth century who was driven insane by visions in the sky during the Battle of Arderydd in 573. Post-Tolkien wizards were apt to be more sarcastic, mercurial, humorous, absent-minded, scruffy, and to wear big, floppy hats. Eventually the wizard evolved into Tom Baker's portrayal of Dr. Who, the all-knowing, eccentric, shape-shifting Time Lord of British television, and fantasy came full circle back to science fiction.

Interestingly, as epic fantasy evolved, the more Tolkien-esque works tended to be based in Celtic myth and legend rather than the Germanic myths that were Tolkien's main inspiration. Part of this may be due to the distinction between strict sword-and-sorcery action-adventure and the more mystical, moral epic fiction. Germanic myths, with their strong Viking element, tended to be more suitable to the action-adventure genre, while the more inward-turning Celtic mythology lent itself better to wish-fulfillment tales of underdog heroes. Whatever the reason, the authors who are often cited as Tolkien-esque, such as Lloyd Alexander, Alan Garner, or Susan Cooper, write fantasies based on Celtic traditions.

Another author often compared to Tolkien is Ursula K. LeGuin, who incorporates her belief systems into her depiction of Earthsea, her own self-consistent world. Stephen R. Donaldson, David Eddings, Katherine Kurtz, George R. R. Martin, Michael Moorcock, Terry Brooks, and Guy Gavriel Kay (who assisted Christopher Tolkien in compiling *The Silmarillion* from Tolkien's papers) are all often mentioned as followers in Tolkien's footsteps as well.

The humorous aspect of Tolkien's dwarves, elves, and hobbits did not go unmined, either. Terry Pratchett's *Discworld* series would not have been conceivable without *The Lord of the Rings* as a paradigm. And then of course there is the classic *Bored of the Rings* (1969) by Henry Beard and Douglas C. Kenney, the parody that was so much fun to write that the authors went on to found the *National Lampoon*.

FROM RINGS TO LIGHT SABERS

It took longer for Tolkien's effect to be felt in film. There was interest in turning *The Lord of the Rings* into a movie within two years of its publication. Tolkien was originally interested in the idea, especially as it was proposed as an animated film, which Tolkien thought was the appropriate medium for this kind of fantasy. However, as with all adaptations of his work, Tolkien had strong objections to the scripts produced.[7] Two animated versions of Tolkien's works appeared after his death, the Rankin and Bass made-for-TV versions in 1978–1980, and the Ralph Bakshi theatrical version, also of 1978. Both were less than critical successes.

Since there was no immediate, direct translation of *The Lord of the Rings* to the screen, the trilogy's influence was indirect, reflected in a slowly growing popularity for fantasy films, as opposed to hard-core rocket-to-Mars or aliens-landed-in-the-backyard science fiction, throughout the 1960s and 1970s. The real impact of Tolkien only emerged with, ironically enough, George Lucas's *Star Wars* trilogy (1977–1983). Although the *Star Wars* movies were set in another galaxy and involved a lot of spaceships, the basic story line was an epic quest, based in a rebellion against an evil empire that destroyed whole planets in its quest for power. Lucas has cited *The Lord of the Rings* as an influence on his conception of his epic, and as the success of *Star Wars* reverberated through the entertainment industry, a spate of fantasies hit the screens. Some of these were pure space opera, but others tracked back to Lucas's mythic sources, inspired by his nod to the influence of Joseph Campbell's *Hero with a Thousand Faces* (1949), and in the process returned to a Tolkienesque take on epic fantasy. (The *Star Wars*–inspired boom in fantasy is as much responsible for the timing of the Rankin-Bass and Bakshi Tolkien movies as the fact that Tolkien was no longer alive to veto scripts.)

One of the problems with fantasy movies is how to tread the fine line between realism and otherness. The popularity of the fantasy genre waxes and wanes with advances in cinematic technology. When the first *Lord of the Rings* movie idea was floated in 1957, the best technology for representing Otherworlds was animation, but animation was associated strictly with children's cartoons; therefore any script for an animated film had to be dumbed down for a perceived juvenile audience. (The Disneyfication of *The Sword in the Stone* in 1963 is a good example, and that came off better than might have been expected.) The animated model special effects typical of 1950s and 1960s movies would not have been able to carry off an entire world in which all of the characters existed in differing scales.

The success of *Star Wars* and its imitators was made possible by another advance in film technology, which allowed Otherworlds to be presented with greater realism. Even so, the construction of simultaneous aliens was too expensive to sustain throughout the entire movie, and was limited at first to show-stopping scenes like the bar in Mos Eisley. (One of the elements Lucas had picked up from Tolkien seems to have been the recognition that different races speak different languages.) As Lucas made his own impact in improving the technology, Otherworlds became more cinematically seamless.

The appeal of *The Lord of the Rings* has always been in its self-consistency, in providing a completely alternative universe that works on its own terms. The problem for films has always been to create something that would not only tell the story, but do so in the same space of suspension of disbelief generated by reading the story. The quantum leap in computer manipulation of images (as well as a willingness to use plain old-fashioned forced perspective) has now made it technologically possible to film a live-action version of *The Lord of the Rings*, which actually has managed to satisfy nearly all Tolkien purists despite the necessity of cutting such well-loved characters as Tom Bombadil and the rewriting of Arwen's role to make her a more prominent character.

THE RETURN OF MYSTICISM

It is a very odd thing that the devoutly Catholic Tolkien should have been an influence on the development of neo-pagan religions in the late twentieth century. While there are numerous lines of influence that converge in one or another of the many neo-paganisms practiced today, many pagans, of whatever persuasion, cite an interest in fantasy literature as children as one of the many paths that led them to their current religion.[8] Fantasy offered visions of alternative universes, models of other ways of existence. Magic is one of the attractions of alternative universes, but what really speaks to most pagans in Tolkien's novels is his depiction of a world where even the rocks are alive, where trees walk and talk, and most importantly, where Nature rebels against its polluters and overthrows its despoilers. Tolkien's attitude was that God created the world, including its humans as well as its animals, plants, and rocks, and that therefore all of God's creations were equally deserving of respect. Tolkien's perception that it is man's duty as the apex of God's creation to be a responsible steward of the environment—to be an environmental Faramir rather than a Boromir, as it were—chimes with the pagan reverence for the earth.

Tolkien's strongest influences on paganism have been through his conception of elves and his use of poetry. From Tolkien's point of view, his incorporation of poems into his epic was inspired by actual medieval prose narratives, which often have poetry inserted in them (as well as the epics, such as *Beowulf*, which actually are poems). The more "Germanic" poems in *The Lord of the Rings*, such as the poems on Théoden's death and Aragorn's recital of the poem on Éorl the Young ("Where now the horse and the rider? ... ") or Gimli's poem on Khazad-dûm ("The world was young, the mountains green"), which are associated with the Rohirrim and the dwarves, tend to be elegiac. In contrast, the elvish poems generally tell mythological stories or legends and have more of a ritual feel to them, as though they are invoking an ongoing process. Although the elves are not portrayed as practicing a religion, their poetry has a liturgical ring.

Tolkien recycled much of the poetry he had written over the last thirty years into *The Lord of the Rings*. Some of it, of course, was poetry he had been writing as part of The Silmarillion and inserted into *The Lord of the Rings* as backstory. The evolution of his poem "Errantry," which was first published in the *Oxford Magazine* in 1933, into the poem "Eärendil was a mariner" sung by Bilbo at Rivendell, is an interesting example of the ways Tolkien would keep reworking a piece of writing until it had turned into something altogether different in meaning, while retaining the same form. Originally a light verse about a man who set out on an errand and got distracted by marrying a butterfly, written in a complex rhythm and rhyme scheme—remember Tolkien's lifelong work on the similarly elaborate *Pearl*—it eventually turned into a mythological poem of how Eärendil obtained a Silmaril and turned into a star in the sky.[9]

The quality of mythic evocation in Tolkien's elvish poetry, as well as the power of its enigmatic sound, seems to be one of the reasons why so many current neo-paganisms draw on Welsh as a ritual language and mythology. It is hard to explain this Cymryphilia any other way—there is no large worldwide Welsh diaspora population (except in Argentina, not noted as a hotbed of neo-paganism), and traces of pre-Christian paganism in Welsh literature are minimal (mostly because the surviving literature itself is minimal). The privileged position of Wales in contemporary neo-paganism can only be laid to the emphasis on Welsh and Welsh-sounding poetry in Robert Graves's *White Goddess* and in *The Lord of the Rings*. After reading Tolkien's poetry, and playing around with the irresistible linguistic information on Sindarin in the appendixes, Welsh will sound very familiar and already have a "magic" aura attached to its sounds.

The elves, especially Galadriel, and the wizards, specifically Gandalf, have also had a significant influence on how pagans conceive of the relation between magic and religion. Elvish magic is an art, the (sub)creation of objects and effects, without the intention of deluding the perceiver. The ability to practice magic is an innate talent rather than a rote application of spells and ritual. This is much closer to the current neo-pagan idea of magic (where rituals are generally believed to raise and focus the innate power within the participants) than the type of ritual magic practiced by nineteenth-century ceremonial magic orders (which generally attempted to compel the deity to follow orders).

HIPPIES AND HOBBITS

It is no coincidence that *The Lord of the Rings* went from best-seller to cultural phenomenon after it was published in paperback in the United States, not because it became cheaper to buy, but because it happened in 1965. The trilogy spoke to a number of emerging cultural trends: The struggle against Sauron echoed growing antiestablishment sentiment, and Frodo's pacifism reflected growing unease with the war in Vietnam. Furthermore, the unequivocal evil of Sauron and Saruman justified rebellion, and the physical manifestation of their evil as pollution and industrialism mirrored increasing concern over the fate of the planet.

Part of the appeal of *The Lord of the Rings* was its depiction of nipping pollution in the bud. Although evil might return in some form, the one thing that is accomplished in *The Lord of the Rings* is that the polluting destructiveness of the Bad Guys is defeated, not once but three times: Isengard is overthrown, the works of Sauron dissolve with the destruction of the Ring, and the Shire is "scoured" (an appropriate term in the context). Pollution may recur, but if it is caught quickly and thoroughly, its effects can be reversed.

Furthermore, the heroes who accomplish this cleansing of the environment are the little guys, literally. The message is that anyone can make a difference. This is, of course, one of Tolkien's main themes, that the small and unregarded peoples of the Earth (Middle or otherwise) can have huge effects. Sauron's biggest error is in assuming that everyone thinks like he does—if Aragorn, or anyone, got their hands on the Ring, they would use it, they would throw their might around, they would want to do everything that he has done but better. Tolkien's mythic struggle between good and evil offered an example of how to attack powerful corporate structures: by thinking differently. This was one of the primary philosophies of the 1960s counterculture, not to "sell out" and think change could be effected by working within the Establishment, but to create completely different structures altogether. These structures included communal living, organic gardening, partnerships without marriage, and food co-ops.

This distrust of the corporate—whether corporate religion, corporate commerce, or corporate government—did not spring directly from reading *The Lord of the Rings*, of course. However, for many people, reading books like *The Lord of the Rings* was what first got them questioning their own world by comparing it with another world. The verisimilitude of Middle-earth, which Tolkien had created through his personal obsession with language and linguistics, carried people into an alternative universe that seemed so real, they wanted to recreate it in their own lives. It inspired them to start thinking of their own alternatives. By a long and twisted route, Tolkien's disgust at the destruction of the trees and countryside of his childhood home at Sarehole in the last years of the nineteenth century has led to demonstrations against the World Trade Organization in the first years of the twenty-first. As Bilbo said, when you step onto the Road, you never know where it will end up taking you.

NOTES

1. Carpenter, *Letters*, 275.

2. Reprinted in J. R. R. Tolkien, *The Monsters and the Critics and Other Essays* (London: G. Allen & Unwin, 1983), 162–97.

3. *Time* (July 15, 1966), 50.

4. Henry Resnik, "The Hobbit-Forming World of J. R. R. Tolkien." *Saturday Evening Post* 239 (July 2, 1966), 94.

5. Carpenter, *Biography*, 149.

6. Carpenter, *Letters*, 377.

7. Carpenter, *Letters*, 260–61, 266–68, 270–77.

8. Graham Harvey, *Contemporary Paganism* (New York: New York University Press, 1997), 182.

9. See Christopher Tolkien, *History of the Lord of the Rings: Part 2, The Treason of Isengard* (Boston: Houghton Mifflin, 1989), 99–109, where he prints the numerous versions of the poem that Tolkien produced, charting its evolution from "Errantry" to the poem that appears in *The Lord of the Rings*.

APPENDIX: THE PUBLISHED WORKS OF J. R. R. TOLKIEN

1. POEMS

1911. "The Battle of the Eastern Field." *The King Edward's School Chronicle* 26, 186 (March):22–27.

1913. "From the Many-Willow'd Margin of the Immemorial Thames." *The Stapledon Magazine* 4, 20 (December):11.

1915. "Goblin Feet." In *Oxford Poetry 1915*, edited by G. D. H. Cole and T. W. Earp, 64–65. Oxford: Basil Blackwell.

1920. "The Happy Mariners." *The Stapledon Magazine* 5, 26 (June):67–70.

1922. "The Clerke's Compleinte." *The Gryphon (Leeds)* new series 4, 3 (December):95.

1923. "The Cat and the Fiddle: A Nursery Rhyme Undone and Its Scandalous Secret Unlocked." *Yorkshire Poetry* 2, 19 (October/November):1–3.

1923. "The City of the Gods." *The Microcosm* 8,1 (Spring):8.

1923. "Enigmata Saxonica Nuper Inventa Duo." In *A Northern Venture: Verses by Members of the Leeds University English School Association*, 15–20. Leeds: Swan Press.

1923. "Iúmonna Gold Galdre Bewunden." *The Gryphon (Leeds)* new series 4, 4 (January):130.

1923. "Why the Man in the Moon Came Down Too Soon." In *A Northern Venture: Verses by Members of the Leeds University English School Association*, 15–20. Leeds: Swan Press.

1924. "An Evening in Tavrobel." In *Leeds University Verse, 1914–1924*, 56. Leeds: Swan Press.

1924. "The Lonely Isle." In *Leeds University Verse, 1914–1924*, 57. Leeds: Swan Press.

1924. "The Princess Ni." In *Leeds University Verse, 1914–1924*, 58. Leeds: Swan Press.

1925. "Light as Leaf on Linden Tree." *The Gryphon (Leeds)* new series 6, 6 (June):217.

1927. "Adventures in Unnatural History and Medieval Meters, Being the Freaks of Fisiologus: (i) Fastitocalon: Natura Fastitocalus." *The Stapledon Magazine* 7, 40 (June):123–25.

1927. "Adventures in Unnatural History and Medieval Meters, Being the Freaks of Fisiologus: (ii) Iumbo, or ye Kinde of ye Oliphaunt." *The Stapledon Magazine* 7, 40 (June):125–27.

1927. "The Nameless Land." In *Realities: An Anthology of Verse*, edited by G. S. Tancred, 24–25. Leeds: Swan Press.

1931. "Progress in Bimble Town (Devoted to the Mayor and Corporation)." *The Oxford Magazine* 50, 1 (October):22.

1933. "Errantry." *The Oxford Magazine* 52, 5 (November):180.

1934. "The Adventures of Tom Bombadil." *The Oxford Magazine* 52, 13 (February):464–65.

1934. "Firiel." *The Chronicle of the Convent of the Sacred Heart (Roehampton)* 4:30–32.

1934. "Looney." *The Oxford Magazine* 52, 9 (January):340.

1936. "Bagme-Blome." In *Songs for Philologists*, 12. With E. V. Gordon, et al. London: University College English Department.

1936. "Éadig Béodhu!" In *Songs for Philologists*, 13. With E. V. Gordon, et al. London: University College English Department.

1936. "The Frenchmen Froth." In *Songs for Philologists*, 24–25. With E. V. Gordon, et al. London: University College English Department.

1936. "From One to Five." In *Songs for Philologists*, 6. With E. V. Gordon, et al. London: University College English Department.

1936. "I Sat upon a Bench." In *Songs for Philologists*, 13. With E. V. Gordon, et al. London: University College English Department.

1936. "Ides Elfsyne." In *Songs for Philologists*, 10–11. With E. V. Gordon, et al. London: University College English Department.

1936. "La Húru." In *Songs for Philologists*, 16. With E. V. Gordon, et al. London: University College English Department.

1936. "'Lit.' and 'Lang.'" In *Songs for Philologists*, 27. With E. V. Gordon, et al. London: University College English Department.

1936. "Natura Apis: Morali Ricardi Ermite." In *Songs for Philologists*, 18. With E. V. Gordon, et al. London: University College English Department.

1936. "Ofer Wídne Gársceag." In *Songs for Philologists*, 14–15. With E. V. Gordon, et al. London: University College English Department.

1936. "The Root of the Boot." In *Songs for Philologists*, 20–21. With E. V. Gordon, et al. London: University College English Department.

1936. "Ruddoc Hanna." In *Songs for Philologists*, 8–9. With E. V. Gordon, et al. London: University College English Department.

1936. "Syx Mynet." In *Songs for Philologists*, 7. With E. V. Gordon, et al. London: University College English Department.

1937. "The Dragon's Visit." *The Oxford Magazine* 55, 11 (February):342.

1937. "Knocking at the Door. Lines Induced by Sensations When Waiting for Answer at the Door of an Exalted Academic Personage." *The Oxford Magazine* 55, 13 (February):18.

1945. "The Lay of Aotrou and Itroun." *Welsh Review* 4 (December):254–66.

1953. "The Homecoming of Beorhtnoth Beorhthelm's Son." *Essays and Studies* new series 6:1–18.

1955. "Imram." Illustrated by Robert Gibbings. *Time and Tide* 36 (December 3):1561.

1962. *The Adventures of Tom Bombadil and Other Verses from the Red Book*. Illustrated by Pauline Baynes. London: G. Allen & Unwin, 1962; Boston: Houghton Mifflin, 1962.

1965. "Once upon a Time." In *Winter's Tales for Children*, edited by Caroline Hillier. Volume 1, 44–45. London: Macmillan; New York: St. Martin's Press.

1967. "For W. H. A." *Shenandoah* 18 (Winter):96–97.

1967. *The Road Goes Ever On: A Song Cycle*. With music by Donald Swan. London: G. Allen & Unwin; Boston: Houghton Mifflin.

2. ESSAYS, SCHOLARSHIP, AND OTHER NONFICTION

1918. "Introductory Note." In *A Spring Harvest: Poems by Geoffrey Bache Smith, Late Lieutenant in the Lancashire Fusiliers*, edited by J.R.R. Tolkien and Christopher Wiseman. London: Erskine Macdonald. Introduction.

1922. *A Middle English Vocabulary: Designed for Use with Sisam's Fourteenth Century Verse and Prose*. Oxford: Clarendon Press. Glossary.

1923. "Henry Bradley, 3 December 1845–23 May 1923." *Bulletin of the Modern Humanities Research Association* 20 (October):4–5. Obituary.

1923. "Holy Maidenhood." *Times Literary Supplement* (April 26):281. Book review.

1924. "Philology: General Works." *The Year's Work in English Studies* 4:20–37. Review essay.

1925. "The Devil's Coach Horses." *Review of English Studies* 1, 3 (July):331–36. Essay.

1925. *Sir Gawain and the Green Knight*. With E. V. Gordon. London: Oxford University Press. Edition, with notes and glossary.

1925. "Some Contributions to Middle English Lexicography." *Review of English Studies* 1, 2 (April):210–15. Essay.

1926. "Philology: General Works." *The Year's Work in English Studies* 5:26–65. Review essay.

1927. "Philology: General Works." *The Year's Work in English Studies* 6:32–66. Review essay.

1928. "Foreword." In Walter E. High, *A New Glossary of the Dialect of the Huddersfield District*, xiii–xviii. London: Oxford University Press. Essay.

1929. "Ancrene Wisse and Hali Meiðhad." *Essays and Studies of the English Association* 14:104–26. Essay.

1930. "The Oxford English School." *The Oxford Magazine* 48, 21 (May):778–82. Essay.

1932. "Appendix I: The Name 'Nodens'." In R. E. M. Wheeler and T. V. Wheeler, *Report on the Excavation of the Prehistoric, Roman, and Post-Roman Sites in Lydney Park, Gloucestershire*. Reports of the Research Committee of the Society of Antiquaries of London, no. 9. Oxford: Oxford University Press for the Society of Antiquaries. Essay.

1932. "Sigelwara Land, Part I." *Medium Aevum* 1 (December):183–96. Essay.

1934. "Chaucer as Philologist: The Reeve's Tale." *Transactions of the Philological Society*:1–70. Essay.

1934. "Sigelwara Land, Part II." *Medium Aevum* 3 (June):95–111. Essay.

1937. "*Beowulf*: The Monsters and the Critics." Sir Israel Gollancz Lecture. *Proceedings of the British Academy* 22, 245–295. London: H. Milford. Essay.

1940. "Preface." In *Beowulf and the Finnesburg Fragment: A Translation into Modern English Prose*, by John R. Clark, revised by C. L. Wrenn, ix–xliii. London: G. Allen & Unwin. Introduction.

1946. "Research v. Literature." *The Sunday Times (London)* (April 14). Review.

1947. "'Iþþlen' in Sawles Warde." With S. T. R. O. d'Ardennes. *English Studies* 28, 6 (December):168–70. Essay.

1947. "On Fairy Stories." In *Essays Presented to Charles Williams*, edited by C. S. Lewis, 38–89. London: Oxford University Press. Essay.

1948. "MS Bodley 34: A Re-Collation of a Collation." With S. T. R. O. d'Ardenne. *Studia Neophilologica* 20:65–72. Essay.

1953. "Form and Purpose." In *Pearl,* edited by E. V. Gordon, xi–xix. Oxford: Clarendon Press. Essay.

1953. "A Fourteenth Century Romance." *Radio Times* (December 4):9. Essay.

1953. "Middle English 'Losenger': Sketch of an Etymological and Semantic Inquiry." In *Essais de Philologie Moderne,* 63–76. Paris: Les Belles Lettres. Essay.

1955. "Preface." In *The Ancrene Riwle,* translated by M. B. Salu. London: Burns & Oates, 1955; South Bend, Ind.: University of Notre Dame Press. Introduction.

1958. "Prefatory Note." In *The Old English Apollonius of Tyre,* edited by Peter Gooden, iii. London: Oxford University Press. Introduction.

1962. *Ancrene Wisse: The English Text of the Ancrene Riwle, Edited from Ms. Corpus Christi College, Cambridge 402.* Introduction by N. R. Ker. Early English Texts Society old series, no. 249. London: Oxford University Press. Edition.

1963. "English and Welsh." *Angles and Britons: O'Donnell Lectures.* Volume 1, 1–41. Cardiff: University of Wales Press. Essay.

1966. "The Book of Jonah." In *The Jerusalem Bible.* London: Darton, Longman, & Todd; Garden City, N.Y.: Doubleday, 1966. Translation.

1969. "A Letter of J. R. R. Tolkien." In William Luther White, *The Image of Man in C. S. Lewis,* 221–22. Nashville. Tenn.: Abingdon Press, 1969; London: Hodier & Stoughton, 1970. Essay.

1975. *Sir Gawain and the Green Knight, Pearl, and Sir Orfeo.* London: G. Allen & Unwin; New York: Ballantine, 1975. Translations.

1979. "Valedictory Address to the University of Oxford, 5 June 1959." In *J. R. R. Tolkien, Scholar and Storyteller: Essays in Memorium,* edited by Mary Salu and Robert T. Farrell, 16–32. Ithaca, N.Y.: Cornell University Press. Essay.

1981. *The Letters of J. R. R. Tolkien.* Edited by Humphrey Carpenter. London: G. Allen & Unwin; Boston: Houghton Mifflin, 1981. Letters.

1981. *The Old English Exodus.* Edited by Joan Turville-Petre. Oxford: Clarendon Press. Edition, translation, and commentary.

1982. *Finn and Hengest: The Fragment and the Episode.* Edited by Alan Bliss. London: G. Allen & Unwin; Boston: Houghton Mifflin, 1983. Essays.

1983. *The Monsters and the Critics and Other Essays.* Edited by Christopher Tolkien. London: G. Allen & Unwin; Boston: Houghton Mifflin, 1984. Essays.

3. FICTION

1937. *The Hobbit: Or, There and Back Again.* Illustrated by the author. London: G. Allen & Unwin; Boston: Houghton Mifflin, 1938.

1945. "Leaf by Niggle." *Dublin Review* 432 (January):46–61.

1949. *Farmer Giles of Ham.* Illustrated by Pauline Baynes. London: G. Allen & Unwin.

1954. *The Fellowship of the Ring: Being the First Part of the Lord of the Rings.* London: G. Allen & Unwin; Boston: Houghton Mifflin, 1954.

1954. *The Two Towers: Being the Second Part of the Lord of the Rings.* London: G. Allen & Unwin; Boston: Houghton Mifflin, 1955.

1955. *The Return of the King: Being the Third Part of the Lord of the Rings.* London: G. Allen & Unwin; Boston: Houghton Mifflin, 1956.

1964. *Tree and Leaf.* London: G. Allen & Unwin; Boston: Houghton Mifflin, 1965.

1966. *The Tolkien Reader.* Illustrated by Pauline Baynes. New York: Ballantine.

1967. *Smith of Wooton Major.* Illustrated by Pauline Baynes. London: G. Allen & Unwin; Boston: Houghton Mifflin, 1967.

1969. *Smith of Wooton Major and Farmer Giles of Ham.* Illustrated by Pauline Baynes. New York: Ballantine.

1975. "A Guide to the Names in *The Lord of the Rings*." In *A Tolkien Compass,* edited by Jared Lobdell, 155–201. La Salle, Ill.: Open Court, 1975.

1976. *The Father Christmas Letters.* Edited by Baillie Tolkien. London: G. Allen & Unwin; Boston: Houghton Mifflin, 1976.

1977. *The Silmarillion.* Edited by Christopher Tolkien. London: G. Allen & Unwin; Boston: Houghton Mifflin, 1977.

1980. *Unfinished Tales of Númenor and Middle-earth.* Edited by Christopher Tolkien. London: G. Allen & Unwin; Boston: Houghton Mifflin, 1980.

1982. *Mr. Bliss.* Illustrated by the author. London: G. Allen & Unwin; Boston: Houghton Mifflin, 1982.

1983. *The Book of Lost Tales, Part I.* Edited by Christopher Tolkien. London: G. Allen & Unwin,; Boston: Houghton Mifflin, 1984.

1984. *The Book of Lost Tales, Part II.* Edited by Christopher Tolkien. London: G. Allen & Unwin; Boston: Houghton Mifflin, 1984.

1985. *The Lays of Beleriand.* Edited by Christopher Tolkien. London: G. Allen & Unwin; Boston: Houghton Mifflin, 1985.

1986. *The Shaping of Middle-earth.* Edited by Christopher Tolkien. London: G. Allen & Unwin; Boston: Houghton Mifflin, 1986.

1987. *The Lost Road and Other Writings*. Edited by Christopher Tolkien. London: Unwin Hyman; Boston: Houghton Mifflin, 1987.

1988. *The Return of the Shadow*. Edited by Christopher Tolkien. London: Unwin Hyman; Boston: Houghton Mifflin, 1988.

1989. *The Treason of Isengard*. Edited by Christopher Tolkien. London: Unwin Hyman; Boston: Houghton Mifflin, 1989.

1990. *The War of the Ring*. Edited by Christopher Tolkien. London: Unwin Hyman; Boston: Houghton Mifflin, 1990.

1992. *Sauron Defeated*. Edited by Christopher Tolkien. London: Harper-Collins; Boston: Houghton Mifflin, 1992.

1993. *Morgoth's Ring*. Edited by Christopher Tolkien. London: Harper-Collins; Boston: Houghton Mifflin, 1993.

1994. *The War of the Jewels*. Edited by Christopher Tolkien. London: HarperCollins; Boston: Houghton Mifflin, 1994.

1996. *The Peoples of Middle-earth*. Edited by Christopher Tolkien. London: HarperCollins; Boston: Houghton Mifflin, 1996.

1998. *Roverandom*. Edited by Christina Scull and Wayne G. Hammond. London: HarperCollins; Boston: Houghton Mifflin, 1998.

FURTHER READING

Annan, Noel. *The Dons: Mentors, Eccentrics, and Geniuses*. Chicago: University of Chicago Press, 1999. A collection of chapter-length biographies of noted Oxford and Cambridge dons (not including Tolkien) mostly from the nineteenth and twentieth centuries. Gives a good sense of university life.

Carpenter, Humphrey. *The Inklings*. London: Allen & Unwin, 1978. The standard biography of the Inklings, written by Tolkien's authorized biographer.

———. *J. R. R. Tolkien: A Biography*. Boston: Houghton Mifflin, 1977. The authorized biography, written with the assistance and blessing of the Tolkien family.

Carpenter, Humphrey, and Christopher Tolkien, eds. *The Letters of J. R. R. Tolkien*. Boston: Houghton Mifflin, 2000. Tolkien's own words.

Chance, Jane. *Lord of the Rings: The Mythology of Power*. Rev. ed. Lexington: University of Kentucky Press, 2001. One of the few book-length works of Tolkien criticism.

———. *Tolkien's Art: A Mythology for England*. Rev. ed. Lexington: University of Kentucky Press, 2001. Looks at Tolkien's relation to mythology and folktale.

Coren, Michael. *J. R. R. Tolkien: The Man Who Created "The Lord of the Rings."* Toronto: Stoddart, 2001. A short biography of Tolkien.

Duriez, Colin, and David Porter. *The Inklings Handbook*. St Louis, Mo.: Chalice Press, 2001. A dictionary-format guide to the Inklings and their works.

Eksteins, Modris. *Rites of Spring: The Great War and the Birth of the Modern Age*. Boston: Houghton Mifflin, 1989. A masterful history of the effect of World War I on literature and the modernist movement.

Fussell, Paul. *The Great War and Modern Memory*. New York: Oxford University Press, 1975. The classic work on the literature and experience of World War I.

Graves, Robert, and Alan Hodge. *The Long Weekend: A Social History of Great Britain, 1918–1939*. New York: W. W. Norton, 1940. A somewhat idiosyncratic view of Britain between the wars by poet and World War I veteran Robert Graves and journalist Alan Hodge.

Grotta, Daniel. *J. R. R. Tolkien: Architect of Middle-earth*. Rev. ed. Philadelphia: Running Press, 1992. A somewhat erratic biography.

Johnson, Judith A. *J. R. R. Tolkien: Six Decades of Criticism*. Westport, Conn.: Greenwood Press, 1986. A very useful annotated bibliography of Tolkien criticism.

Knight, Gareth. *The Magical World of the Inklings*. Shaftesbury, Dorset: Element Books, 1990. Focuses on the lives and works of Tolkien, Lewis, Williams, and Owen Barfield.

Shippey, T. A. *J. R. R. Tolkien: Author of the Century*. Boston: Houghton Mifflin, 2001. A well-informed critical evaluation of Tolkien.

———. *The Road to Middle-earth*. Boston: Houghton Mifflin, 1983. Probably the best book of Tolkien criticism available; thoroughly explains Tolkien's philological and mythological influences.

White, Michael. *J. R. R. Tolkien*. Indianapolis: Alpha Books, 2002. A biography that adds little to Carpenter but includes interesting readings of Tolkien's works.

INDEX

About the Author

LESLIE ELLEN JONES received her Ph.D. in Folklore and Mythology Studies from UCLA in 1992. She has published essays on many aspects of Celtic mythology, and the representation of folklore and mythology in film and television. She is the author of *Happy Is the Bride the Sun Shines On: Wedding Beliefs, Traditions, and Customs, Druid Shaman Priest: Metaphors of Celtic Paganism*, and *Myth and Middle-earth: Exploring the Medieval Legends Behind J. R. R. Tolkien's Lord of the Rings* (forthcoming). She also designed and taught The Lord of the Rings: J.R.R. Tolkien, Mythmaker, a twelve-lesson course for Barnes & Noble Online University, www.bn.com.